The Ancient World

LONGMAN SECONDARY HISTORIES

R. J. Cootes and L. E. Snellgrove

The Ancient World

R. J. COOTES

and

L. E. SNELLGROVE

LONGMAN

LONGMAN GROUP UK LIMITED
Longman House, Burnt Mill, Harlow,
Essex CM20 2JE, England
and Associated Companies throughout the world.

First published 1970
Fourteenth impression 1987

Produced by Longman Group (FE) Ltd
Printed in Hong Kong

ISBN 0-582-20503-4

Contents

Preface

This book is designed to provide an introductory history course during either the whole or a major part of the first year in the secondary school. Great care has been taken to keep its language simple, in view of the wide range of reading attainment found in unstreamed classes. The scope of the book is wide, partly because of the nature of the subject, partly to give both teacher and pupil as many 'starting points' as possible.

The authors consider the Ancient World a suitable first year course for two main reasons. First, knowledge of its chief characteristics is an essential preliminary to the study of later ages, containing as it does basic ingredients of Western civilisation like Greek ideas of government and philosophy, Roman ideas of law and imperialism and Jewish conceptions of God. Second, the authors' experience of teaching this age group convinces them that it is a period which such pupils find interesting.

Basically, the authors have tried to produce a clear, general account of those features of the Ancient World which can be understood by eleven or twelve-year-olds. But at the same time they have attempted to look more closely at certain aspects so that these 'come alive' for the reader. This technique is, of course, used by teachers in the classroom, because a close look at any 'patch' of history is nearly always more interesting than mere generalisations.

At best, general textbooks are a springboard for more thorough study. The authors wish this book to be viewed as such and hope it will prove useful. Finally, they would like to thank Mrs. Madeleine Gunny for her tireless efforts in collecting the pictures, and their wives for sustained help and encouragement.

R. J. Cootes
L. E. Snellgrove

March 1970

Acknowledgements

The publishers are grateful to the following for permission to reproduce photographs:

Aerofilms Ltd.: 17, 164 (top), 171, 188–9; American School of Classical Studies, Athens: 91 (bottom); Athens National Museum: 80; Barnaby's: 56–7, 69, 81; Berlin Staatsmuseum: 30; Boston Museum of Fine Arts: 58, 75; British Museum: 10, 14, 22–3, 39, 68, 75 (bottom), 82, 86, 88, 91, 94, 96, 99, 106, 113 (top), 122, 133, 137, 144 (bottom), 160, 164, 166, 172, 187, 190–1; British Museum (Natural History Museum): 2, 3, 4; British Travel Association: 179; Ny Carlsberg: 131; J. Allan Cash: 118; M. Cass: 18, 135 (bottom), 144–5, 162; Grosvenor Museum Chester: 128; Chesters Museum, Hexham: 182, 184; China Missionary Society: 60; China Welfare Institute, Peking: 54; Colchester Museum: 186; Freeman: 42; Giraudon: 25, 64, 135, 146; Glastonbury Antiquarian Society: 9; Green Studio, Dublin: 16; Guildhall Museum: 169, 180, 186; C. Hallward: 78; André Held: 6–7, 34, 62, 97, 98, 110; Hirmer Verlag: 24; A. F. Kersting: 36, 92, 113, 172; Miss Kathleen Kenyon: 8, 10 (top); Keystone Press: 48–9, 77, 92, 111, 134, 139, 140, 143, 151; Professor Leakey: 3 (top left); Magnum Photos: 117, 148, 155, 173, 177; The Mansell Collection: 72–3 (2 pictures), 85, 104–5, 114, 120–1, 143, 147; The owners of Petworth Place: 174; Philipons Ltd.: 185; Pictorial Colour Slides: 176; Picturepoint: 153; Paul Popper: 12; J. Powell: 132, 158; Arthur Probsthain: 47; Radio Times Hulton Picture Library: 132 (left); Rainbird: 32, 33 (2 pictures), 37; René Roland: 29; D. Samuel and H. Gottesman: 66–7; Oscar Savio: 149; Scala: 125, 142, 163; Dr. J. K. St. Joseph: 170, 181, 192; The Science Museum: 175; The Sunday Times: 183; Graham Tingay Esq.: 162 (top), 165; Washington Gallery of Art: 59; Sir Mortimer Wheeler: 45; Roger Wood: 35, 66, 126–7, 130, 150, 152, 154–5.

The photograph on the cover is reproduced by permission of André Held.

We have been unable to trace the copyright holder of the photograph on page 138 and apologise for any breach of copyright.

Part 1
The Beginnings of Civilisation

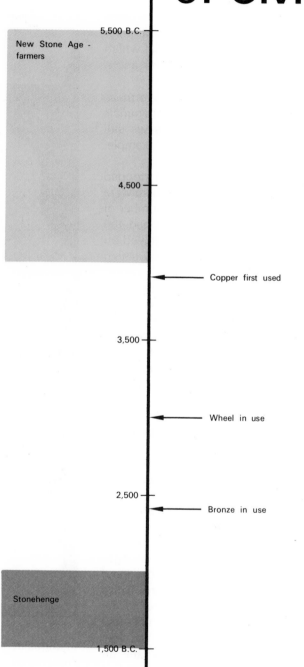

5,500 B.C. —

New Stone Age -
farmers

4,500 —

← Copper first used

3,500 —

← Wheel in use

2,500 —

← Bronze in use

Stonehenge

1,500 B.C. —

1 Uncivilised Man

Man belongs to the animal family known as Primates. His nearest relatives are the three large apes (gorilla, chimpanzee, orang-utan) and the smaller gibbons. All these animals are tailless and most prefer to live in trees. He is also a mammal, which means an animal which breast feeds its young. Mammals have lived on the earth for about 160 million years.

At first mammals were in danger from large reptiles. When these huge creatures died out about sixty million years ago, mammals increased their numbers rapidly. Some grew into animals we still know, the horse, giraffe, whale, elephant, lion and wolf for example. Others lived in trees and developed into apes.

About twenty-five million years ago certain types of ape stopped living in trees. Why they did this we do not know. Possibly there were less trees available because of drier conditions. A certain number of ape families did remain in the forests, where they developed the powerful arms of the present-day animal. But other types stayed on the ground, so their legs became stronger. Gradually these walking apes grew less like animals and more like men.

One family, called hominids, were like men and may have been the ancestors of *Homo Sapiens* (Wise Man) as modern man is called. Their arms were still long and their foreheads sloping. But their brains were larger than other apes, they walked on two legs more often than four and used their fingers and hands to grip things. Hominids lived as late as 25,000 years ago and man probably learnt many skills from them.

Man the adaptor

Various experts tell us about these early people. Anthropologists study the skeletons which have been found. They show us how man changed physically during this period. Archaeologists dig into mounds of dust in caves and villages to find the bones, tools and weapons used by them as they developed. Even today there are peoples in Africa, Australia and the Arctic who still live in the same primitive way as early man, so we can learn a lot from them.

Much has been discovered but much remains a mystery. Nobody knows where the first Homo Sapiens lived. During the Ice Ages large glaciers caused the water level of the oceans to drop. Land 'bridges' appeared connecting North and South America and North America and Asia. Consequently mammals were able to wander far and wide over the earth and ape men followed them in search of food. In 1959 the skeleton of a hominid nearly two million years old was discovered in Olduvai Gorge, Tanzania, Africa. Four years later an even older ape-man was found at Fort Ternan in Kenya. From this it seems possible that man's original home was Africa.

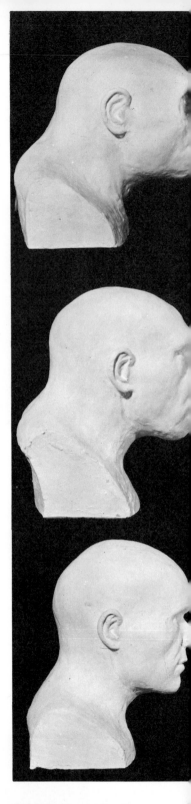

Changes in skulls of Primates over 600,000 years.
The bottom one is *Homo Sapiens*

Some stone tools; left to right, an advanced hand axe, a cutting blade, and an early hand axe

An early woman probably looked like this

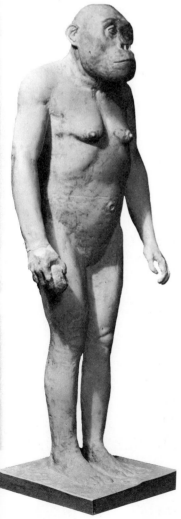

At some time after he came down from the trees man began to walk on his hind legs. Thus, his front limbs with their useful fingers were free to do other things. After many thousands of years this allowed him to invent and use tools. Other animals have only natural equipment, claws, teeth, paws and hair. Man was able to scratch the ground with picks, shovels and axes or skin an animal to make a separate hairy coat for his own body. There are great advantages in this. A shovel or axe can be replaced if broken. An artificial coat can be taken off if it becomes warm. In other words, these inventions allow man to adapt himself to changing conditions. This is one reason for his success compared with other animals.

Man the toolmaker

Man's first tools were of stone. The oldest known camp containing stone tools has been found at Olduvai Gorge in Tanzania. Here, about two million years ago, pebbles were collected and used to break things. Of course, such pebbles were not always the right shape. Their smooth surface could not scrape vegetation from the ground very well or cut a tree branch. So men began to chip flakes off their pebbles in order to give them a sharp or rough edge. Pebble-tools have been found in South Africa, Portugal and western Asia.

About 100,000 years ago different tools began to be made for special purposes. Hand axes seem to have been the earliest kind. Then pointed tools were made for digging and boring; long choppers with sharp edges for cutting. Such axes and choppers were first found in northern France. Later, archaeologists found them in many parts of Europe, Asia, Africa and India. Few of them had handles; they were probably wrapped in grass to give protection for the hand. Between 50 and 30,000 years ago men fitted handles to their stones, thus making two-part tools. They invented the sewing needle, the shape of which is still the same today. They also discovered how to make fire, either by rubbing two sticks together or twisting one stick round and round in a hole full of wood shavings. Fish were caught with spears and harpoons and a heavy stone pick was designed to dig up roots and make holes.

Man the talking animal

Such inventions were the result of working together. This co-operation was forced on man by his weakness compared with other animals. Only a gang of men could hope to trap and overpower a woolly rhinoceros or a mammoth (a large elephant with huge tusks). Only a family could protect human babies during the long years when they were small and helpless. Yet because he sheltered in tribes and families man eventually became more powerful than the animals who threatened him. It was another example of adapting himself to overcome difficulties.

Co-operation was helped by talking. Men have powerful larynxes and strong tongue muscles. For this reason their throat sounds are more varied than those of other animals. Different noises could be used to indicate different actions or things. These gradually grew more complicated until they became a language. This was important for two reasons. First, it meant that men could understand each other far better than most animals seem to do. Quite difficult commands and instructions became possible. Second, language made men think. Words not only express thoughts; they help create them. Most thinking is done with words even if they are not spoken. In fact, really advanced thinking would be impossible without words.

In this way man gradually overcame his weaknesses. He became a talking, thinking animal.

A mammoth. It was found preserved in ice

2 Hunters and Artists

For at least a million years man had only stone tools and weapons. This 'Stone Age' can be divided into two parts. At first, Stone Age man hunted for his food, either by picking berries and fruits or by killing animals. This food-gathering time is called the Old Stone Age. Later, certain peoples discovered ways of growing cereals and taming animals. This farming period is termed the New Stone Age. Of course one Age did not follow another in every part of the world. Some kept to the old ways, and hunters and farmers often lived quite near each other. Indeed, in parts of Malaysia, Africa and Australia there are tribes who still live as Stone Age hunters.

Stone Age hunting was tough and dangerous. In parts of Europe and Africa it was possible because there were few trees at this time and large numbers of animals roamed over the plains. Day by day small parties of wild men followed the herds of bison, horses, deer and mammoth. It seemed an unequal contest. Mammoths could crush men to pulp under their feet. Horses and deer could run faster. But man used his superior brain to overcome his prey. He dug pits for animals to fall in, or lured entire herds towards high cliffs. He made poisons and dipped his arrow-heads in them.

Frequently a hunt became a slow, terrifying struggle. A wounded creature might injure many hunters. It might take days to die slowly of poison or grow weak in the bottom of a pit. But man won more battles than he lost. More often than not the tired hunters returned to their cave with a dead animal which would supply meat, fat and fur. The earliest cave home of this sort has been found in China, at Chou-Kou-Tien near Peking.

After the meal, bones and broken stone weapons were often thrown into the back of the cave. The dust settled on them. Today archaeologists dig through the layers of rock and soil in such places. They know that the remains at the bottom must be older than those at the top. In this way they discover which tools and weapons were made and used first.

Cave drawings

Faced by such enemies, man turned to magic for help. Away in some deep cavern, pictures of the creatures he wished to kill were drawn on the walls. Stone Age carvings were first discovered in the south of France about a hundred years ago. Workmen digging to lay a railway line found a large drawing of a mammoth. It was an exciting moment because before that time only pieces of its bones and teeth had been found. No one had ever seen such a creature. A few years later a little girl was walking through some caves at Altamira in Spain when her candle light revealed red and white pictures of bison. 'Toros' (bulls), she shouted excitedly to her father. Soon afterwards experts came to examine them and found many more examples of Cave-man art.

These drawings probably remained undiscovered because they were difficult to reach. Some are at the end of narrow tunnels. Others are behind underground lakes or springs. In such secret places, the wizard-artist, using stone tools and hair brushes, drew and painted the beast required by the hunter. Often he created the scene which his men desired. A bison would be shown dying of wounds. Sometimes internal parts such as the heart or stomach were drawn outside the animal to show that those were the places the hunter must aim for. Deer would be drawn swimming a river because animals are easier to catch at such times. Most of the drawings were accurate; perhaps dead animals were dragged into the chamber and used as models. Most are in large caves whose hardened clay floors occasionally show footprints. This means possibly that the hunters danced before the pictures as a way of making the magic work.

Working by the light of burning fat in a stone lamp, such men produced the earliest known art. The oldest are merely scratched outlines. Later ones are coloured black, white, brown, red and yellow. Rubbing bowls were used to break up the colouring materials or even to mix colours with fat. Colours were sometimes painted by hand or brush. They were also sprayed on by blowing through a piece of hollow bone. Great care was taken. Small pieces of bone have been found which have drawings scratched on them. These were either practice pictures or examples to teach some pupil.

The first art

The results are often beautiful and they show that the artists took pleasure in what they were doing. At Montignac in France a large oval-shaped cave contains carvings so life-like that they seem about to move. At Altamira a dying bison is shown, sagging as he is hit by many arrows. Modern lights reveal all his agony, shown clearly in the delicate red, yellow, white and blue shadings on his body.

The men who drew him never saw him properly because of poor lighting. Possibly he looked even more mysterious in the flickering half-darkness. In a way these caves and their drawings are the first temples. The artists who drew the animals were really priests, who did not hunt but were allowed a share of the food their 'magic' produced. The place itself was rarely changed and one picture was often drawn on top of another.

About 10,000 years ago a warmer climate caused forests to cover some of the plains. Larger animals could not survive in such conditions. They wandered elsewhere or died out. Cave-man magic no longer produced a successful hunt so the artist-wizards gave up their work. Men moved away to fresh water where they hunted wild fowl or fish. The caves grew empty and silent until their beauties were discovered in recent times.

Mankind has never completely lost the taste for hunting. For centuries it was the sport of kings and nobles. Even today many people like to fish, shoot or chase the fox. There was excitement as well as danger in the life of the Old Stone Age.

Cave painting of a bison
from Altamira, in Spain

3   Farmers of the New Stone Age

The change from hunting to farming was almost certainly due to women. In the Old Stone Age they had spent their time looking after children and collecting seeds, herbs and berries for food. As they did so some must have noticed how the seeds were blown by the wind, covered with dust and made to grow by the sun and rain. What was to stop them scratching a hole with a stick and planting seeds themselves? So farming started, probably in western Asia where wheat and barley grow wild.

Near Mount Carmel in Israel archaeologists have found skeletons lying beside horn sickles (curved knives for cutting ripe wheat). Round their skulls were shell headbands. Round their necks were rough strings of beads. Here were some of the earliest farmers. One can imagine the hunters scoffing at such pitiful gardening. Hunting was a wild, free life. Who wanted to sit at home with the women and watch plants grow? Nevertheless, farming leads to a more settled and less primitive way of life. A hunter must be on the move, following the herds. A farmer must stay by his crops so that he can harvest them. Hunting is basically an animal way of living. Farming is a step away from being a mere animal. It leads to civilisation as we know it.

A flint sickle found at Jericho

As the herds grew less and the climate drier, many hunting families gathered near water to find other ways of living. No longer could they wander in small parties over the plains. Instead they settled together near a river, lake or oasis. A number chose the coastal plains of Greece, Turkey, Persia and Syria. Others lived near great rivers like the Nile in Egypt, the Indus in India or the Tigris and Euphrates in Mesopotamia.

Once farming had begun it led to quick changes. New Stone Age people broke up the ground with pointed sticks. They reaped cereals with sickles made from pieces of flint embedded in wood or even an animal's jawbone. They brought water from the river in pots to refresh the soil. They dug ditches or put up fences to protect their growing crops and lived near them in houses of mud brick. And although the men in particular must have found farming boring after hunting, they also discovered that it produced a more regular food supply. Fewer people died of starvation and the population increased.

Early villages

The earliest known example of a food-producers' village, dating from 8000 B.C., has been unearthed at Shanidar in northern Iraq. A more famous one is the oasis village settlement near Jericho in Israel. This covers eight acres and is surrounded by a ditch 9 feet deep and 18 feet wide. It was probably inhabited from about 6000 B.C. Houses were made of pressed mud; later, bricks were used. As

well as these hill settlements, there were also villages near lakes and rivers. In Europe wood was used for buildings. Some were even built in the water on stilts to ensure safety from attack. Lakeside villages of this type existed in Switzerland. Similar ones are inhabited today in New Guinea.

Collapsed walls of a hut from a lake village in Somerset, England

The New Stone Age was a time of great achievements. Every nourishing food plant, including wheat, barley, rice, millet and maize, was first grown by *Neolithic* peoples. They learnt how to separate wheat from the husk, how to rub grain between two stones and how to brew beer and make wine. They made the first early attempts to measure time in order to know when to plant their seeds. In the next section we shall read of one particular method they used. They also began to harness their animals with the yoke to use them for work.

New discoveries

Early men discovered two ways of measuring the seasons. Some calculated the time it took the moon to circle around the earth and divided time into these twenty-nine to thirty day periods. They did this by watching the moon at night and called such periods months, meaning moonths, or 'moontime'. Others worked out how long it took the earth to move around the sun, although in fact, they thought the sun moved around the earth.

The Solar (Sun) year of $365\frac{1}{4}$ days is the more accurate of the

Two pots from the New Stone Age

This fat mother goddess was found in a flint mine

two and it is essential if man is to keep track of the seasons. The Lunar (Moon) calendar will not agree with this because there are actually $12\frac{1}{3}$ lunar months in a Sun year. Consequently a moon calendar has to be adjusted with twelve and thirteen month 'years' to keep it in time. Only the Egyptians and the Jews discovered a workable sun calendar. All other ancient peoples used a lunar one.

Neolithic people were the first to tame animals. This domestication, as it is called, probably occurred first in western Asia where there were many wild goats and sheep. It was as important a step forward as the discovery of how to grow crops. The Old Stone Age hunter only caught meat and skins. He could not milk the animals he hunted, or use them to pull and carry. Both these improvements were possible with cattle, sheep and horses. Some New Stone Age people became herdsmen and shepherds. Unlike crop farmers, these men wandered from place to place seeking fresh pastures for their herds and flocks.

Settled life in one spot also encouraged women to experiment more. They already knew how to plait twigs and rushes to make baskets. Now they rubbed rough wool into thread and interlaced it to make woollen cloth, or did the same with flax reeds to make linen. They fashioned wet clay into crude pots which when baked in a kiln (oven) could be used to store food. So pottery and weaving were born.

The Great Mother

Old Stone Age hunters had hoped magic would help them in their quest for food. Being fierce and warlike it is possible that their idea of god was of a man-like hunter. New Stone Age farmers were even more dependent on nature. The genuine magic of rain and sun working on the soil was essential if their crops were to grow. Unlike the hunter, they came to look upon the earth as a sort of woman, whose body gave forth harvests even as a real woman gives birth to babies.

The earliest known forms of religion reveal men worshipping a Great Mother. For example, in Egypt there was Hathor, the Cow-Goddess, and in Sumeria, Ishtar. Later such goddesses were thought to have god-lovers who died each winter and were reborn each spring, just like the crops. This is probably why most primitive religions demanded the yearly sacrifice of a person or animal. Were not the seeds buried in order that they might grow? So something of their own, something precious, must die if the goddess was to be pleased.

The great improvements of the New Stone Age were not shared by all. Some tribes were still able to hunt, and sometimes they attacked and destroyed farming communities. In later times many wars were caused by hunters and shepherds conquering farmers. On the other hand, the two may sometimes have helped each other. Pots and shells have been found in New Stone Age villages thousands of miles from where they were made. From this it seems likely that hunters acted as traders, carrying goods from village to village and even from one country to another.

4 The Fertile Crescent

Stone Age people needed to catch or grow enough food to live. Only one or two important persons, a priest or artist in each community, could be spared to do anything else. Then, as methods of farming improved, there was food left over. It is on this surplus supply of foodstuffs that more complicated ways of life have been built. A man who does not have to spend all his time cultivating cereals, or hunting, can do other things. He may fashion tools or weapons as a full-time job. He may study the stars, design buildings or invent machinery. As he does so he and people like him will gather together in settlements larger than villages. When this happens life has started to be civilised; the very word 'civilisation' comes from the Latin *civis* meaning citizen or town dweller.

The Fertile Crescent

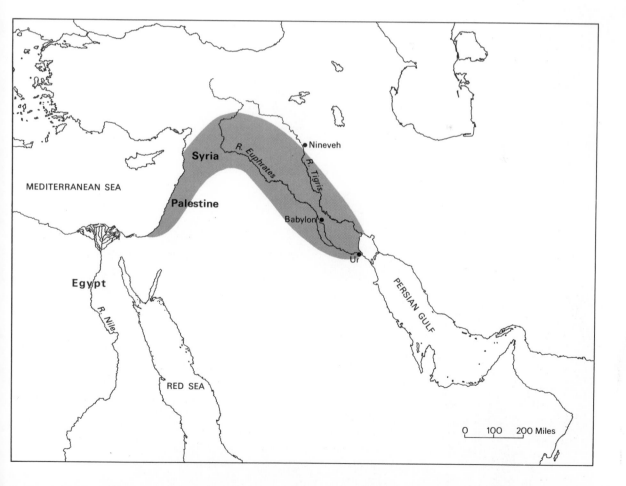

Shadoofs were used for watering the land. They are still in use today. Here is a double one used to lift water to a great height

Favourable conditions for large-scale food production first occurred in an area stretching from Egypt through Palestine and Syria to the rivers Tigris and Euphrates. Because of its shape it is called the Fertile Crescent. Today much of this land is a pathless desert. In ancient times there was more rainfall, so cereals, dates, figs and olives were grown, especially as water could be obtained from oases and rivers. Small wonder that people multiplied in this land, filling the valleys with their towns and temples.

No animal lives in this way but the town organisation which developed did resemble the life of bees, ants and wasps. Like these insects, who are governed by queens and divided into workers and non-workers, the early cities were ruled by a priest-king and his nobles. Very often the monarch was regarded as a god and all the houses were built around his temple-palace.

Irrigation

Of course, new inventions and ideas were needed to take full advantage of this opportunity. Control of water was the main problem. During most of the year there was little rain. Then there would be a very wet season which often led to sudden floods. The art of dealing with these difficulties is called irrigation and it was essential to these first civilisations. At times of drought it was necessary to store water and to carry it to the parched fields. Canals and channels were dug from the river, storage tanks built and earth dams constructed in special spots. Fields were cut into hillsides like giant steps which sloped inwards. Such *terracing* meant that the water would not run away too quickly. Lifting pots of water was a hard task but the *shadoof*, a long pole with a bucket on one end and a heavy weight on the other, made it easier to lever up water supplies. During times of flood, ditches or pipes were used to drain the extra water away. In later periods, rivers were trapped or diverted and cuttings made in hillsides.

The rich black mud left after a river flood produced better crops than ordinary soil, especially if it was dug before planting. These people discovered that it could be broken up more effectively if the tool had a long handle attached to it. Such a plough penetrated deeper if it was pulled by a rope tied to the horns of an oxen. Irrigation systems, plus the shadoof and plough, changed farming in another way. Such tough work needed a man's strength. It could no longer be done entirely by women.

The carrying of grain for storage and water for irrigation meant increased use of animals. Horses, asses and camels were loaded with sacks and pots or made to pull wooden sledges. Early people probably got the idea of wheels from the common practice of rolling objects on tree-trunks. By 3000 B.C. wooden wheels made in three pieces and fixed together with pegs were in use in the Middle East.

Storage of water and food made pots essential. At first they were slowly shaped by hand. Then someone discovered that if wet clay was thrown on to a turning wheel it could be fashioned in a few minutes. So the potter's wheel, like the shadoof and the plough, aided human progress.

The age of metal

The change from stone to metal benefited mankind enormously. Metal is far better than stone for making tools and weapons. It is as hard as stone yet it can be melted, bent and shaped. If broken it can be repaired.

How metal was first discovered will never be known for sure. But the tale told by the Ancient Egyptians is probably near the truth. It is said that some travellers who camped for the night banked up their fire with pieces of rock. Next morning tiny beads of copper were found in the ashes. This was because the heat had melted the copper in the rocks. After this had happened many times men understood exactly what had occurred and began to melt copper deliberately.

Once men realised how useful metal was they worked hard to master it. Such mastery involved various processes. Copper needs to be well hammered before it can be used. For harder metals, furnaces were necessary to obtain greater heat. Metal working of this sort was a full time job. A person who could melt metal, shape it with hammers, mix it and pour it into moulds, was an expert. He had no time for other work. Copper was the first metal to be worked successfully. This was followed in some parts by the use of bronze, which is a mixture of copper and tin. Iron was discovered later and is the hardest of all. It made such hard swords that tribes were forced to use it or be beaten in battle.

Man cannot live without water. Most Old Stone Age villages were built near it. In India, China, Asia, Africa and Europe early man lived where there was fish and wild fowl, where travel was made easier by boat or canoe, where sharp river bends or marshlands made it difficult for enemies to attack. In later ages, farmers had to be near water if their crops were to grow. For this reason the Fertile Crescent became the cradle of civilised life. In the next four sections we shall read about these so-called Riverene Civilisations.

An early iron sword. Its
scabbard (case) was made
of bronze

5 The Spread of Farmers and Metalworkers

The more settled ways of farmers and metalworkers spread only slowly from the Middle East. As a result, European and African tribes were just starting to farm when people in the Fertile Crescent were digging irrigation systems and building cities, temples and pyramids.

This map shows how the arts of agriculture and metalwork spread from their original home. For Europeans the most important route was the River Danube. This great waterway ran through fertile valleys from the Black Sea to Germany. Spain, parts of France and Britain were probably influenced via the Mediterranean and Atlantic

Routes showing the spread of farming and metalworking

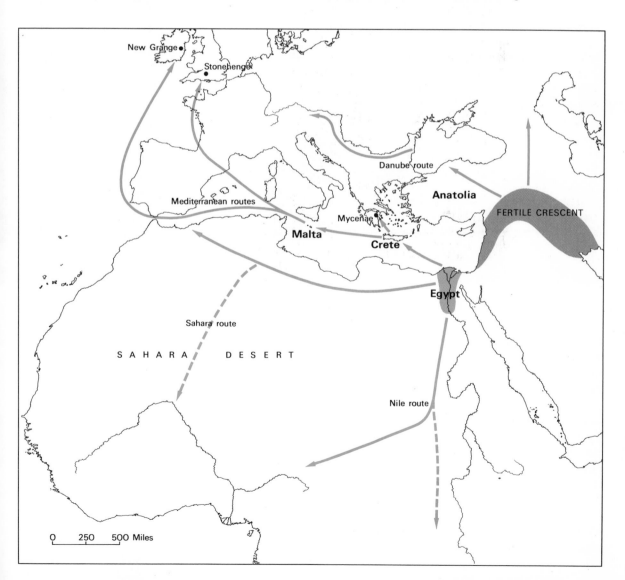

A room inside the stone tomb at New Grange in Ireland

coast. Africa may have been affected from two directions. To the west, the river Nile flows into the heart of the continent. Further east, there may have been a 'Sahara route' because this part of Africa was not the waterless desert it is today.

Working like detectives, archaelogists have patiently traced these routes across thousands of miles by collecting tiny bits of evidence. To such experts there are plenty of remains which tell a story. Sometimes a complete settlement is found. More often odd tools, pots or bones give clues. For example, if a grindstone or sickle comes to light, or a pot shows the faint mark of a corn grain, it is clear that the early settlers at this particular spot were corn-growers.

Graves are good finds because most early men believed in an after-life similar to this world. Therefore they buried the corpse with objects needed in the next world—with clothes, weapons, pots and

jewellery. Later we shall read of a famous Egyptian tomb of this kind. And because death was thought to be important, they made their tombs into land-marks. Early Europeans dug mass graves made up of a number of passages and rooms; a house of the dead in fact. Such rock tombs were often formed from rock slabs which were covered with earth. Examples can still be seen in Malta and at New Grange in Ireland as well as in many parts of Britain and Europe.

Occasionally such great stones (megaliths) were grouped to form large temples for religious worship. The best known is Stonehenge on Salisbury Plain in southern England.

The giant's dance
Many tales have been told about these mysterious objects. The most famous is that of Geoffrey of Monmouth, a 12th century writer.

Stonehenge from the air: notice the bank and ditch, the outer circle of stones, and the two horseshoe shapes in the middle. The Heelstone is at the top of the picture. (When this picture was taken experts were putting back some of the stones. You can see the scaffolding they were using)

A connecting stone that has fallen from the top of Stonehenge

According to him, an ancient British king, Aurelius Ambrosius, wished to build a memorial to some of his warriors killed in battle. The wizard Merlin told him of a set of magic stones in Ireland called the Giant's Dance. Aurelius sent an army to Ireland led by his brother. It defeated the Irish and with the help of Merlin's magic brought the stones to Salisbury Plain. Certainly the stones stand in patterns which suggest magic. Indeed, the larger stones were called Sarsens—meaning Saracens or foreigners—because our ancestors thought that a race of giants had put them up.

An outer circle of sarsens, weighing 45 tons each and standing 30 feet high, surround an inner circle of bluestones, 5 feet high. Inside these two circles are two sets of stones arranged in horseshoe shapes, an outer one of big stones enclosing one of bluestones. Surrounding the whole area is a circular bank and ditch. The tops of the outer circle were once connected by slightly curved stones. The inner circle was made up of Trilithons, that is, of three stones arranged to form gateways. Most strange is a circle of holes dug inside the first circle and a single stone outside called the Heelstone (Sunstone).

Some of the questions about Stonehenge have been answered. The ditch is merely the space caused by taking earth to build the bank. The sarsens probably came from a quarry just twenty miles away at Marlborough Down. As many as a thousand men may have been needed to drag each one of them on sledges. The smaller stones are not found in this part of England. The nearest bluestone quarry is in South Wales, over 135 miles away as the crow flies. It is possible they were dragged by sledge to Milford Haven, paddled by canoe up the Bristol Channel and pulled overland to Salisbury Plain. This is a journey of 240 miles. To go to such trouble may mean that these stones were thought to be magic.

The builders

Who built Stonehenge? It was begun by New Stone Age workmen in about 2000 B.C. and completed by Bronze Age people about 500 years later. The nearest equivalent stone ring is in Malta. Therefore it is possible that some master builder from Crete, Mycenae or Malta was brought to England to see that the work was done properly. And recently a Mycenean dagger was found carved on one of the stones. More interesting still is the question, why was it built? For many years it was thought to be a temple of the fierce priests known as Druids. Others thought it was a large and important cemetery.

We now know it was neither. Almost certainly it was a temple connected with the seasons because the Heelstone is in a direct line with the sunrise on June 21st—midsummer's day in the Northern Hemisphere. However, what festivals took place, or what exactly was worshipped there, will probably never be known for sure. Yet Stonehenge can still tell us a lot. Better than anywhere else in Europe or Africa, it shows us the work of a strong, wealthy and determined people who, although thousands of miles from centres of civilised life, were able to copy much of the skill of such far off races.

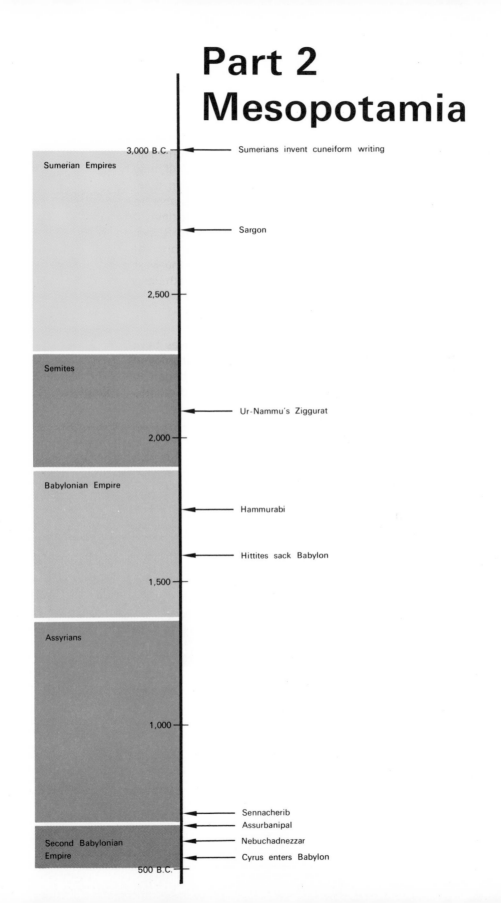

Part 2
Mesopotamia

3,000 B.C. — ← Sumerians invent cuneiform writing

Sumerian Empires

← Sargon

2,500 —

Semites

← Ur-Nammu's Ziggurat

2,000 —

Babylonian Empire

← Hammurabi

← Hittites sack Babylon

1,500 —

Assyrians

1,000 —

← Sennacherib
← Assurbanipal
Second Babylonian
Empire
← Nebuchadnezzar
← Cyrus enters Babylon

500 B.C. —

6   Sumeria and Babylon

Two rivers, the Tigris and the Euphrates, rise in the Armenian mountains and flow into the Persian Gulf. As they near the Gulf, they move closer together. The fertile mud plain formed between them has been given many names. The ancient writers called it Sumer; in the Bible it is referred to as the Plain of Shinar. Until recent times it was known as Mesopotamia, meaning the Land between Rivers. Now it is called Iraq. This land has seen many civilisations. At different times, wandering tribesmen living in the deserts to the west and cave-dwellers from the mountains of the east have been attracted to it.

The Sumerians

Sometime between 5,000 and 3,500 years before Christ was born (B.C.) mountain folk speaking a language called Sumerian moved into the plain. At first they were still hunters. Then they began to control the river floods, building earth banks, channels and ditches

The Middle Eastern Empires

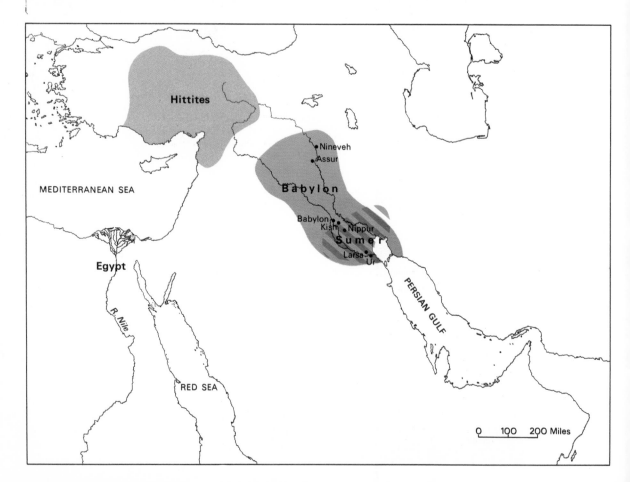

This tablet in *cuneiform* writing talks about the chances of a sick man recovering or dying, and the chances of victory or defeat in war

to direct the water where they wanted it to go. Irrigation was the basis of all Mesopotamian farming. Only occasionally did either river break its banks and cause disaster. The memories of such happenings probably led to the story of the Flood mentioned in the Bible.

Mesopotamian towns developed from separate clusters of dwellings around temples to the gods. For this reason a group of people was sometimes named after a city, not a country. For example, Babylonians were from Babylon and Assyrians from Assur. The Sumerians founded towns at Ur, Kish, Larsa and Nippur. They became very skilled, building houses of sun-dried mud, growing wheat, barley, vegetables and dates, spinning and weaving cloth, and slicing up tree trunks to make some of the first wheels.

They also invented a form of writing. This development is very important. Writing makes it possible for men to send messages when apart and even to read the thoughts and ideas of the dead. A great deal of knowledge is stored and passed on to later peoples in this way. Sumerian writing was scratched on soft clay with a triangular-

shaped nib. This nib made wedge-shaped signs which are·now known as cuneiform from the Latin word for wedge, *cuneus*. For nearly two hundred years scholars worked at translating various types of cuneiform carved on stones, but these were not completely understood until 1857.

In about 2300 B.C. the Sumerians were conquered by their northern neighbours, people speaking a language called Semitic.

'The Standard of Ur'. It is made of bitumen (a sort of tar) with stones inlaid, and shows a banquet with courtiers drinking to the sound of music. In the centre servants are leading

bullocks and lambs to be killed; at the bottom men are carrying heavy bundles which may be goods captured in war

These Semites were probably closely related to the Sumerians and they are the ancestors of the modern Jews and Arabs. A Semitic conqueror named Sargon seems to have controlled most of Mesopotamia. A later king, Ur-Nammu (2113–2096 B.C.) ruled a prosperous empire. To show his wealth and power he built a very large *ziggurat*. This was a pyramid-like temple, popular since the earliest times in that area. Its centre was an earth mound, enclosed by a sloping wall

200 feet long and 8 feet thick. Leading to the top were three stairways of one hundred steps each, topped by a single flight which led to the part sacred to Nannar, the Moongod.

The Ziggurat of Ur-Nammu

The rise of Babylon

These early Semitic kings were overthrown by another Semitic people, the Amorites, who used a strange animal from the grasslands north of the Caspian Sea. They called it 'the ass of the mountains' and employed it to pull their war chariots. We know it today as the horse. The Amorites broke through the line of fortresses meant to keep them out and easily defeated armies untrained in chariot fighting. By 1894 B.C. they were on the banks of the Euphrates building Babylon. This city was situated where the two rivers were only forty miles apart. It was easy for its citizens to control most of the trade routes leading to the Black Sea and Syria, Palestine and Egypt. They became rich and prosperous and are usually known as Babylonians.

The Babylonians were a clever people whose ways have influenced present-day life. They were among the first to use money as an alternative to swapping goods (barter). Lumps of silver of a given weight represented the articles to be exchanged. For example, a sack of corn was said to be worth so many *shekels* (ounces) of silver. Using the cuneiform script, they were pioneers of arithmetic. The idea that a number changes its value if moved left was theirs, but with them it meant it was multiplied by sixty not ten.

For some reason they liked to count in twelves. This is why today we still reckon in dozens, divide a day into twenty-four hours and a minute into sixty seconds. To them the number seven was lucky, probably because they worshipped seven planets. This began the custom of having a week of seven days which to the Babylonians were known as Shamash, Sin, Nergal, Nabu, Marduk, Ishtar and Ninib. The Jews copied this seven-day week. So did the Saxons and Vikings, although they named them after their gods. These are the names we use today.

7 Hammurabi's Laws

Between 1792 and 1750 B.C. the Babylonians were ruled by a powerful king called Hammurabi. He collected many laws and customs of the Mesopotamian lands and had them carved on stone pillars for his people to read. Whether they were always obeyed is not known. Indeed the only pillar ever found had been stolen by raiders from a neighbouring country. Nevertheless, Hammurabi's laws tell us much about the way of life of his people.

A Mesopotamian ruler was looked upon as a steward or manager who ran the country for the gods. Hammurabi's laws begin with this statement: 'When Marduk commanded me to give justice to the people of the land and to let them have good governance, I set forth truth and justice throughout the land and prospered the people.' The pillar has 3,600 lines explaining 282 laws. The inscriptions end with sixteen lines of blessings for those who obey the laws and 280 lines of curses for the disobedient.

This is part of the only Hammurabi column ever found. It shows Hammurabi receiving the laws from the sun-god, who holds a ring and a staff

'An eye for an eye . . .

The Mesopotamians believed in taking revenge for wrongs. If a member of a family was killed by another, the two families would often take a life for a life until hardly anyone survived. Governments tried to stop such blood feuds by carrying out revenge for the injured person themselves. As a result, the basis for Hammurabi's laws was 'an eye for an eye and a tooth for a tooth'. For instance, one states, 'if a man has made the tooth of another fall out, one of his own shall be knocked out'. If a house fell down and killed the owner, the builder was executed. Furthermore, if the house fell down and killed the owner's son, the builder's son was killed. Occasionally such rules varied a little. A criminal could sometimes pay a fine to the wronged person or family. A slave who struck his master lost his ear not his hand. This was because a slave without an ear was more use than one without a hand.

A great many laws concerned farming. All sorts of rules were made about ownership of land, the type of rent to be paid and so on. There were penalties for not clearing out channels or ditches, which show how important irrigation was to the farmer. It was also considered necessary to punish shepherds who let their sheep damage crops. A special section dealt with the growing of date palms, because this tree was put to many uses. Besides providing food, wine, vinegar and honey, its fibres were used for baskets, its date stones for fuel, and its wood was the only timber available in Mesopotamia.

Ancient and modern

Some laws seem sensible, others strange by today's standards. Women were quite well protected. Some could even own property — a rare thing in the ancient world. But a man could divorce his wife if she had not borne him a son. This he did merely by saying solemnly, 'you are not my wife'. A person accused of witchcraft was forced to jump into the Euphrates. If he drowned he was guilty; if he floated he was innocent. This was cruel but more sensible than the system in England many centuries ago where you were guilty if you floated and innocent if you sank! Punishments were severe. A man who wrongfully accused another of murder was either drowned, burned or fixed on a wooden stake. A burglar who had burrowed into a mud house through the wall was hanged where he had entered.

Other laws sound most modern. On rivers, boats propelled by oars had to give way to those sailing before the wind, rather as powered boats and steamers have to give way to yachts today. The Mesopotamian method of ploughing with two oxen yoked one in front of the other meant more work for the rear beast. So a farmer who hired a young animal and used it at the rear instead of the front was fined. He could also demand compensation if the ox attacked him. Nor would modern people quarrel at the rule that a doctor could charge ten shekels for curing a rich man but only five shekels for curing a poor one. Less well-off people were generally given protection under these laws.

8 The Assyrians

The Babylonians were threatened by fierce enemies. One of these, the Hittites, came from Armenia. In those remote mountains they had found a way of getting a fire hot enough to melt iron. Therefore, they had iron weapons which were much tougher than the bronze ones used by the Babylonians. They were able to capture Babylon in 1595 B.C. although they were driven out. Then the secret iron making process was also discovered by an even more warlike people living around Assur in the Tigris Valley. It was these Assyrians who destroyed the first Babylonian state.

The Assyrians were the most cruel people of ancient times. Using foot soldiers, horsemen, chariots and even warships they captured town after town and showed no mercy to their captives. Rival kings were blinded or burned alive. Men, women and children were massacred or sold into slavery. Of one conquest the most powerful Assyrian king of all, Assurbanipal, boasted, 'For a distance of a month of twenty-five days' journey I devastated the land of Elam.

The Assyrian Empire

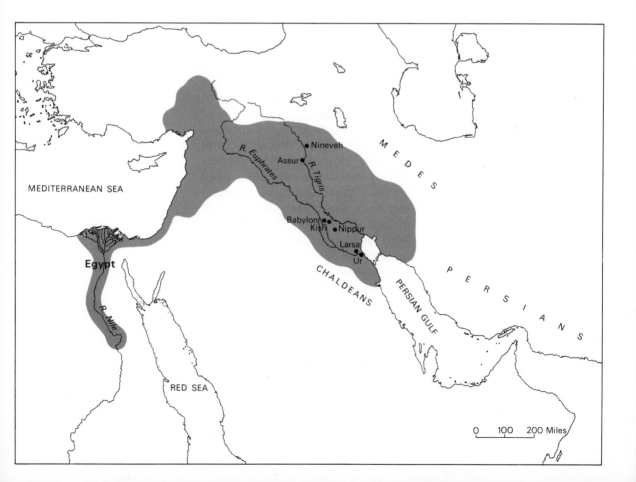

The noise of the people, the tread of cattle and sheep, the glad shouts of rejoicing, I banished from its fields.'

At first Babylon tried to be friendly with Assyria and to help in her wars. Then in 689 B.C. the Assyrians turned against them and attacked the great city itself. For nine months the Assyrian King Sennacherib besieged the town. When at last he captured it he had it utterly destroyed. Even the mud banks controlling the Euphrates were broken so that much of the city was flooded and turned into a swamp.

The glories of Nineveh

Even so, there was a more pleasant side to these fierce rulers. Sennacherib, for example, was very interested in farming and engineering. His capital, Nineveh, received water from a 300-yd. long aquaduct (bridge to carry water) built by his engineers. His fields were irrigated with the help of shadoofs, and he seems to have introduced cotton growing to Assyria. Under his rule Nineveh became a splendid city with a big park and graceful squares shaded with trees. Its temples to the gods resembled ziggurats. Its palace walls were decorated with colourful tiles and guarded by gigantic statues of winged bulls with human heads. Clever carvings of men and animals filled his palaces.

Assurbanipal was interested in education. At Nineveh he collected a library of 22,000 clay tablets written in cuneiform script. Some of these 'books' told stories of the Creation of the World and the Flood. Others were about medicine, science and mathematics. There was even a dictionary. These books were not just for show. The man who boasted how he had destroyed Elam, described himself like this: 'Marduk, master of the gods, granted me as a gift a receptive mind and ample powers of thought. Nabu, the universal scribe, made me a present of his wisdom, . . . I have solved the laborious problems of division and multiplication, which were not clear.'

Unfortunately for the Assyrians, they had made too many enemies. Long years of war killed off their best warriors and forced them to rely on foreign soldiers who fought only for money. Their frontiers had no natural barriers, no mountains or deserts, so they had to keep on conquering people to make them obey. When weaker kings began to rule, two races, the Medes and Chaldeans, decided to attack. Assur fell in 614 B.C.; Nineveh two years later. The Assyrians received a terrible dose of their own medicine. After three months' fighting, Nineveh's walls collapsed because of the high floods. The beautiful temples and palaces were destroyed. Sennacherib's efficient irrigation system was ruined and farming on the banks of the Tigris returned to a Stone Age level.

Second Babylonian Empire

Babylon's glory was restored by the Chaldeans. During the time of its most successful king, Nebuchadnezzar, it was ringed by two 60-feet high walls stretching for eight miles. A moat encircled it, nearly 300 feet wide in places. Inside were mighty ziggurats and gateways and a wonderful line of man-made terraces on which there was enough earth for trees, plants and flowers to grow.

These 'Hanging Gardens', so called because they were so high they seemed to hang in the air, were one of the wonders of the ancient world. Of them a Greek wrote, 'This wooded enclosure was square in shape with sides four hundred feet long and sloped like a hillside with terrace built on terrace as they are in a theatre. During the building of the terraces galleries were built underneath them which carried the entire weight of the gardens. . . . On this was piled earth, deep enough to contain the roots of the largest trees and when it was levelled over, the garden was planted with all sorts of trees which would appeal to those who saw them either by their great size or by the beauty of their appearance.' Machinery raised water from the river to the garden and some of the galleries were made into apartments for the king and queen.

This winged bull with a human head once guarded the doors of the Assyrian palace at Nimrud. Bulls like this can be seen at the British Museum

The glory of this second Babylonian empire was ended by the Persian king, Cyrus the Great. In 547 B.C. he moved through Syria into Asia Minor. The last Babylonian king is supposed to have been feasting when the Persian attack began. So unprepared were the Babylonians that there was little fighting. In October 539 B.C. Cyrus entered Babylon to be greeted by cheering crowds who waved date palms. The days of independent Mesopotamian kingdoms were over.

The Ishtar Gate at Babylon. It was covered with richly-coloured bricks

Part 3
Egypt

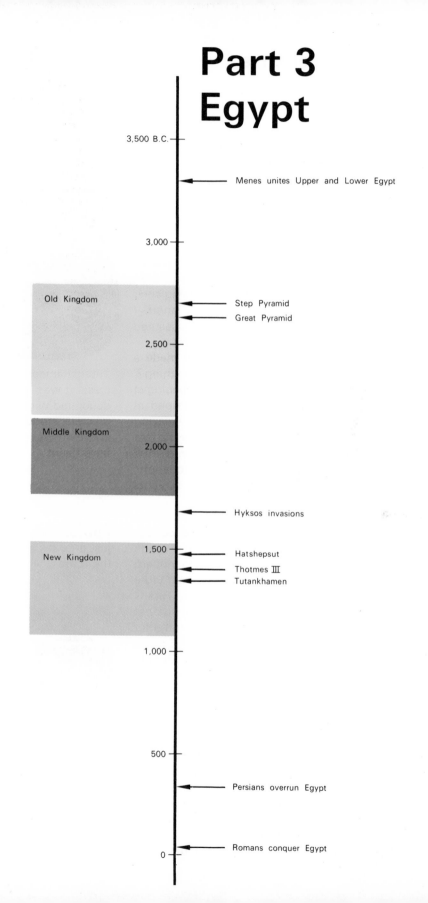

3,500 B.C.

Menes unites Upper and Lower Egypt

3,000

Old Kingdom

Step Pyramid
Great Pyramid

2,500

Middle Kingdom

2,000

Hyksos invasions

New Kingdom

1,500

Hatshepsut
Thotmes III
Tutankhamen

1,000

500

Persians overrun Egypt

0

Romans conquer Egypt

9 Tutankhamen's Treasure

In November 1922 an archaeologist, Howard Carter, was digging in the valley where the Ancient Egyptians had buried their pharaohs. Most of the royal tombs had been robbed of their valuable treasures centuries before. One, that of the boy king Tutankhamen, had never been found. For five years Carter had searched, hoping to be the first to open it. Now he seemed very near success. Underneath the burial chamber of Pharaoh Rameses VI a door had been discovered. Although shut, it had obviously been opened by robbers and then resealed. Perhaps they had been captured or disturbed forcing their way in. This door proved disappointing but behind it lay another passageway and door. On this door the seal of Tutankhamen seemed intact. Carter was about to open a tomb shut for 3,270 years.

To prevent fresh air destroying everything inside, Carter made a tiny hole and pushed a candle through. 'Can you see anything?' asked his companion, Lord Carnarvon. For a time the archaeologist was too surprised to speak. 'Yes, wonderful things,' he gasped at last. In the flickering candle-light was revealed the most amazing find from the ancient world. Piled in a room 26 feet long by 12 feet wide were nearly 60,000 objects which Egyptians believed their pharaoh would need in the next world. Gold couches, chariots, painted boxes, furniture and gold statues of the king and his servants filled the room.

Tutankhamen's funeral mask. It was made of gold decorated with semi-precious stones. The king is shown wearing his false beard

Nearby was a second room which contained the king's body, enclosed in four gold coffins. It was decorated with gold collars, rings and bracelets. On his face was a life-like gold mask. By his side lay his daggers. Nothing like this had ever been discovered in modern times. Small wonder the world went wild at the news. Women wore Egyptian style clothing, popular songs were written about Tutankhamen and a record was made of a soldier blowing a war trumpet from the burial chamber. To hear this strange, unearthly sound after so many centuries thrilled people and helped to make one of Egypt's most unimportant rulers more famous than its greatest kings. People who knew little about history became interested. Who were these Egyptians who could bury a young king with such riches?

Howard Carter, left, pictured just after his entry into the tomb

The inundations

About 10,000 years ago, the climate of the Mediterranean area seems to have changed. Less rain fell and wandering tribesmen were forced to move to the nearest water supply. The Nile is the largest river in North Africa. As it nears the sea it spreads out to form a great delta. Each year, at certain seasons, heavy rains in central Africa swell its waters and cause it to spill over the land. When such a flood goes down it leaves miles of thick mud ideal for growing crops.

The first people to gather by its banks were not farmers. They con-

tinued to hunt for food and clothing, chasing the hippopotamus and crocodiles through the marshy reeds. By 3500 B.C., however, their descendants had invented the plough and settled down as farmers, relying on the river to water their crops. In such a hot, dry land this would have been impossible without the yearly flooding. Each year people watched anxiously for signs of a rise in river level. They discovered that floods normally occurred a few days after the star Sirius had appeared at dawn in the summer sky. When this happened, they made the happy day the first of their New Year. Indeed, the Egyptian Sun calendar of twelve months of thirty days each with five extra days at the year's end, grew from such flood calculations. Once the inundation or flood began, special stones called 'nilo-meters' measured it. Afterwards the black mud gave forth such good harvests that Egypt became known as the Black Country.

Further upstream the deserts are closer to the river bank so there is less land for farming. For this reason the first civilised area was the Nile delta, or Lower Egypt. The southern valley was settled later and was called Upper Egypt. A King Menes of Upper Egypt united the two parts in about 3300 B.C. He conquered the delta and founded the city of Memphis. Because there had originally been two Egypts, the pharaohs wore a double crown, the high white crown of Upper Egypt and the red one of Lower Egypt. Eventually the country was divided into forty-two provinces, ruled by the pharaoh, his priests and thousands of lesser officials.

Pharaoh as god

The pharaoh was very important to the Egyptians. Not only was he their priest and king. He was also a god and his personal name was too sacred to be even spoken. This is why he was called 'pharaoh' which means 'the Royal House' or family. All important religious festivals were conducted by him. At such times he would appear in public carrying a carved shepherd's staff, dressed in a gold apron or kilt and wearing an artificial beard fixed to his face by a strap.

In early times he was carried on a throne but after horses were introduced into Egypt (about 1500 B.C.) most pharaohs preferred to ride in chariots. On stone carvings they were shown standing proud and erect, as though always young and strong. When death came to them, the Egyptians believed that they were not judged like ordinary men. Instead they went straight to heaven, sailing across the sky in a sunboat driven by golden oars. One such boat had been found in the tomb of Tutankhamen.

Tutankhamen, dressed for a religious festival

An eagle: one of the king's jewels

10 Religion

Burial customs played an important part in Egyptian religion. When an Egyptian died it was believed that his body and soul parted. The body was preserved as a mummy. The soul was in two parts, called Ba and Ka. Ba was the soul bird who could take any shape and fly anywhere. Ka resembled the dead person exactly. Powerful men like nobles or pharaohs were supposed to have more than one Ka. Carvings nearly always show a Ka standing behind a pharaoh, protecting him. Most souls had to go on a long journey after death. Ideas about this varied. Sometimes it was a ladder leading to the underworld; on other occasions it involved a boat trip. Afterwards the soul was judged by the god Osiris. Good people went to paradise. Evil ones had their hearts torn out by a monster.

Osiris was believed to have been killed and brought back to life.

A woman giving a present to the god Osiris who is about to judge her.

This is why he ruled over the dead. Other powerful gods were Ra, the Sungod, Isis, the wife of Osiris, and Horus, who was really two gods. As god of heaven Horus was shown as a hawk whose eyes were the sun and moon and whose wings reached the ends of the earth. There was also a Horus who was the son of Isis and Osiris. Later Amun, the Sungod of the priests of Thebes, became more important than Ra.

Only one pharaoh, Amenhotep IV, ever tried to change Egyptian beliefs. He decided that there was only one god whom he called Aten. Aten's sign was the sun and the pharaoh became his high priest. He changed his own name to Akhenaten, meaning 'It is pleasing to Aten' and composed beautiful poems like this in his honour:

> Thy dawning is beautiful in the horizon of heaven
> O living Aten, beginning of life!
> When thou risest in the eastern horizon of heaven
> Thou fillest every land with thy beauty,
> For thou art beautiful, great, glittering, high over the earth
> Thy rays, they encompass the lands, even all thou hast made.

These were sung, like psalms, in his temples. Unfortunately, this annoyed the priest of Amun in particular and after Amenhotep's death all traces of this worship were wiped out.

Mummies

Egyptians liked to preserve the bodies of those they loved. Since Egypt has a dry climate and its soil contains preservatives like resin (a kind of gum) and bitumen (a sort of tar) this was not difficult. After death the brains and other organs were removed and placed in special jars. The heart and kidneys were left in the body. What happened then depended on how rich the dead person had been. A poor person was merely enclosed in a thick layer of bitumen to keep out the air. Rich corpses were carefully wrapped in yards of linen bandage. This was criss-crossed in pleats leaving diamond-shaped spaces which were decorated with precious stones and pieces of gold.

Special care was taken to preserve the face so that the soul would recognise its own body. For the same reason a mask of the face was made and fitted on top. Sometimes the embalming or mummifying process took months. The mummy of a nobleman would probably have its skin coloured, its neck filled out and artificial eyes fixed in the eye sockets. Finally it would be drawn to the Nile on a sledge and ferried by boat to the House of the Dead on the western bank. This was a desert area used for burials because it was unfit for farming.

Pyramids

The simplest Egyptian stone tombs were square and flat topped. These were called *mastabas* from the Egyptian word for a bench. About 3000 B.C. King Djoser decided to be buried in a tomb made of six mastabas of decreasing size placed one on top of the other. The

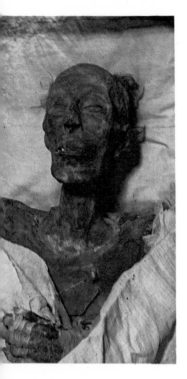

Mummy of Rameses VI. You can still see the bandages wound round his fingers to preserve them

result was the Step Pyramid at Zakkarah which is 200 feet high. Later pharaohs filled in the steps to form a continuous sloping surface. There is one like this at Meidum built for King Snofru. His son Khufu (Cheops) designed a true pyramid and it was erected at Giza.

This Great Pyramid consists of more than two million blocks of limestone and granite. Each side is 755 feet long and it rises to 480 feet. It was built by laying a base and then dragging the stones up special earth ramps. Nearby stands another pyramid built by Khafra, Khufu's son. This is guarded by the Great Sphinx, a statue with the face of Khafra and the body of a lion. Inside both are numerous chambers and passages. Some shafts point up to the sky and may have been used to study the stars. Unfortunately such large buildings attracted robbers who found the bodies and took the valuables away. For this reason later pharaohs preferred to be buried in the Valley of Kings, a deserted spot in the Western Desert.

Whatever his rank, however rich or poor, an Egyptian believed in another life after death, provided he had pleased the gods. In every case, he expected the same position he had enjoyed in this world. A workman was buried with his tools. A rich lady would be surrounded with jewellery and bracelets. A king was entombed with his treasures and with tiny models of his servants.

Khafra's pyramid. It is the one with the cap of marble still in place. The other large pyramid is that of Cheops.

11 Life and Laws

A scarab used in an ornament

So much of what we know about the Egyptians concerns the dead that it is worth remembering that they were gentle people who loved life and most living things. Although they were keen hunters, they were very fond of keeping pets. Cats were loved almost as much as human beings. When a favourite one died the whole family went into mourning and it was mummified like a human corpse. Dogs, rather like modern greyhounds in appearance, were kept as pets or as guards for the house. Even the dung beetle, or scarab, was honoured because it rolled its ball of dung along in the way Egyptians believed the gods rolled the sun across the sky. Gold models of scarabs were very popular as ornaments throughout Egypt.

Poorer people lived in one-storey brick or mud buildings with roofs of palm leaves. A rich man's home might consist of a number of two-storey buildings. These were usually built around a sheltered garden because Egypt is a very hot country and shade is important. A large house might have as many as seventy rooms, and gardens with several hundred trees to provide cover. Flowers were particularly popular and Ancient Egypt's national flower, the lotus, was worn by women in their dresses and hair. Ladies' clothing was simple—just a long linen dress made from the flax which grows in the Nile delta. There was no need for thick clothing in such a country and wool was despised as a coarse material difficult to clean.

Rich women were heavily made up. Eyebrows and eye lashes were painted dark blue, lips were coloured and rouge put on the cheeks. Men wore a loin cloth held up by a belt. Noblemen dressed in pleated kilts and flowing robes. They shaved both their head and beard. Since sweating was a problem even men wore perfume. There was also a curious custom of placing a small cone of fat on the head. As it melted it sent a sweet-smelling trickle of liquid down the forehead and cheeks.

Art and education

The Egyptians were fine craftsmen. They turned pottery on wheels and baked their clay in an enclosed furnace instead of an open one. They also made objects in copper, bronze, gold, silver and iron. Their workmen were able to carve not only wood but precious stones and they almost certainly invented glass. Indeed, their glassware was admired and copied all over the ancient world. Although clever at stone-carving, Egyptian artists did not attempt to draw absolutely life-like pictures. For example, people were often carved with their heads sideways (in profile) but their bodies facing the front. Ship drawings often show all the oars on one side. Even so, such pictures tell us much about Egyptian life, dress and customs.

It was natural that such clever people should value education.

By 2430 B.C. at the latest they had devised a form of picture writing called *hieroglyphics* (sacred carved letters). Originally each picture indicated a word but gradually it came to represent a letter. A man was thought to be well educated if he could copy this writing really well. Such a scholar wrote on paper made from lengths of papyrus reed stuck together in a criss-cross fashion and stored in rolls. A brush reed dipped in ink made from soot, water and gum was used to write. Egyptians thought such writing was very important. They believed that if they used the right sentences or phrases on a tomb or wall they could please the gods and get what they wanted. For everyday life, however, few could afford the time for this complicated writing so a quicker version called *hieratic* (priest writing) was developed. Busy traders later produced a simpler version still called *demotic* (popular script).

The Rosetta Stone

For centuries writing experts wondered what such characters meant. Then in 1799 two French soldiers in Egypt found a stone near Rosetta. Carved on it were words in three scripts, hieroglyphic, demotic and Greek. Since Greek was understood it was possible to compare them all. Careful study by Champollion, a French scholar, revealed the Egyptian letters for 'Ptolemy' because the writing was a record of honours given by priests to pharaoh Ptolemy Epiphanes. Later the letters of the word 'Cleopatra' were made out from a similar stone. Gradually it became possible to translate the many papyrus rolls and stone carvings which had survived and so to learn about Egyptian history.

Egyptian schools were probably very tough places by modern standards. An old Egyptian saying goes like this, 'The ear of the boy is on his back and he hearkeneth when he is beaten'. Nevertheless only well educated men could hope for high positions in the government, so it was worth suffering as a child. Schools taught mathematics and astronomy as well as writing. The Egyptians were able to make one of the first Sun calendars because they knew so much about the movement of the sun and planets. Healing was also considered important. Schools of medicine were established at Said, Thebes and Heliopolis. Doctors spent a lot of time trying to cure eye complaints caused by the swarms of flies in Egypt. They sometimes used quite modern methods but more often they relied on spells and magic.

Laws were carried out by lawyer-priests who served Maat, the goddess of justice. Trials were well organised with a judge and a clerk who made notes of what was said. Accused persons were allowed to speak in their own defence. Serious punishments were usually decided by the pharaoh. They ranged from death to loss of limbs or hands and beating for lesser crimes. Egyptian laws were regarded as fair by other ancient peoples. The great Hebrew law giver, Moses, was educated at the Egyptian court so he must have known something of the country's laws.

The Rosetta Stone. The hieroglyphic writing is at the top; then comes demotic script and finally Greek

12   Hatshepsut's Voyage

Because the Egyptians were a river people their chief form of transport was the boat. Just as after death many were ferried across the Nile for burial, so in life they spent many hours on its waters, either for pleasure or work. Land travel was hot, dusty and tiring. It was much better to row or sail on the Nile's cool waters. Originally Egyptian boats were merely bunches of reeds tied together at each end. Then larger craft were made, some with a platform inside to stop the sailors getting too wet. The bunched reeds at either end pointed upwards, giving the vessel a half-moon shape. Wooden ships were made in this shape later.

Egypt has few tall trees. The most common tree, the acacia, gives only short lengths of timber. Thus Egyptian ships had no long tree trunk (or keel) on which to build the hull. Instead small pieces were pegged or bound together on a frame, rather as bricks are laid on a wall today. To give added strength, a cable of doubled rope was tied to each end and supported along the deck on wooden holders like props for a washing line. Occasionally this was twisted tighter to prevent the hull sagging at either end. It seems a clumsy and fragile way to make a ship. In fact it produced a fast craft which often survived sea storms because its frame could give before a wave.

Egyptian sailors made many long voyages, both across the Mediterranean and into the Red Sea by way of an ancient canal which ran from the Nile. The most famous expedition was that sent by Queen Hatshepsut to Punt (probably Somalia). This first Queen of Egypt sent eight such vessels and they were large enough to bring back much cargo, including 3,300 cattle and thirty-one myrrh trees. The sweet smelling myrrh trees were particularly welcome because they do not grow in Egypt.

Hatshepsut had all the trees planted in the grounds of her great temple at Der-el-Bahri. On its walls her sculptors carved a picture of one ship and wrote this underneath: 'The loading of the ships very heavily with marvels of the country of Punt: all goodly fragrant woods of God's land [the East], heaps of myrrh resin with fresh myrrh trees, with ebony and pure ivory, with green gold of Emu, with cinnamon wood, with two kinds of incense, eye cosmetic, with apes, monkeys, dogs and with skins of the southern panther, with natives and their children. Never was brought the like of this for any king who has been since the beginning.'

When the horse became known in Egypt, chariots and two-wheeled carts were used as well as boats. No horses were ridden but poor men sometimes travelled astride donkeys. However, boats were always more important. It was in a boat, not a chariot, that the Egyptians imagined their pharaohs voyaging to heaven. Unfortunately much of this temple was destroyed after Hatshepsut's death.

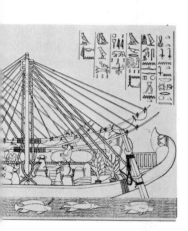

Wall carving at
Der-el-Bahri showing one
of the ships which made
the journey to Punt

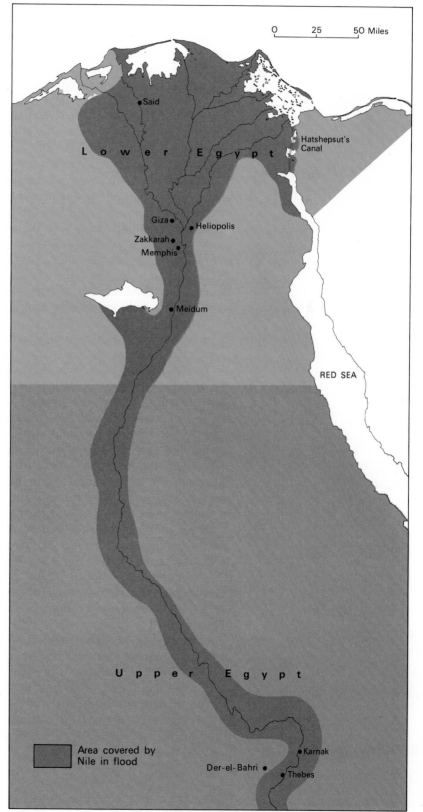

0   25   50 Miles

Said

L o w e r   E g y p t

Hatshepsut's
Canal

Giza
Heliopolis
Zakkarah
Memphis

Meidum

RED SEA

U p p e r   E g y p t

Area covered by
Nile in flood

Karnak
Der-el-Bahri
Thebes

Ancient Egypt

Old and Middle Kingdoms

Egypt's history was affected by two things. First the country was cut off from surrounding peoples by desert and mountains. These natural boundaries protected it for many centuries and limited the number of foreign invasions. Only when transport improved was Egypt seriously threatened and finally conquered. Second, the country's strength or weakness depended upon the character of the pharaoh. If he was strong willed Egypt usually prospered; if not, the country became disorderly with rival groups of priests quarrelling. The earliest period, called the Old Kingdom, was a time of peace and it left the pyramids as a memorial to future ages.

The Old Kingdom collapsed in a series of rebellions against various weak pharaohs. Different and stronger royal families (dynasties), gradually gained control. Most famous of these were the pharaohs of the eighteenth dynasty who transferred Egypt's capital to Thebes and made it the most wonderful city in Egypt. Here they built the largest of all Egyptian temples, that of Karnak on the east bank of the Nile. Its great pillars still stand and some are so thick that one hundred men could stand on top of each. The long rule of the eighteenth dynasty is called the Middle Kingdom and it was a time of great prosperity. The Suez canal used by Hatshepsut's ships was dug from the Red Sea at this time, although it later silted up. Trade expanded and beautiful shrines and temples were built.

The Middle Kingdom was destroyed by foreign invaders. In about 1670 B.C. a mysterious people from Asia swept into the country. Egyptians called them the Hyksos, meaning either 'Shepherd Kings' or 'Rulers of the Uplands'. Little is known about these warriors except that they fought in chariots drawn by horses. After nearly a century of fighting they were expelled but the years of resistance had made the Egyptians a much more warlike people. In later centuries Egyptian armies, equipped with chariots and armed with bows, arrows and axes, were conquering an empire which at one time stretched from the River Euphrates to the Sahara Desert.

Their most successful leaders were military-minded pharaohs like Thotmes III, Seti and Rameses the Great. Thotmes fought seventeen campaigns in Syria and the temple at Karnak was enlarged to celebrate his victories. Many pointed columns (obelisks) are carved with the story of his battles. One is well known to English people because it was brought to Britain and placed on the Thames Embankment in London. It is called 'Cleopatra's Needle' but has nothing to do with that queen.

Ancient Egypt was not rich enough to wage such wars for long. About 1000 B.C. movements of population all over the Mediterranean area upset trade and led to frequent famines in Egypt. Nevertheless, Egypt remained independent until 341 B.C., when it was overrun by the Persians. It continued to be very important, with its own rulers, until the Romans conquered it in the reign of Cleopatra (69–30 B.C.).

Cleopatra's Needle on the Thames Embankment, London

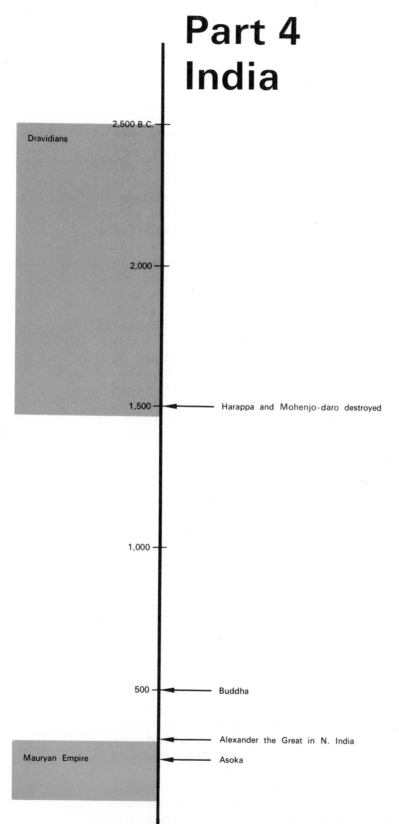

Part 4
India

2,500 B.C.

Dravidians

2,000

1,500 ← Harappa and Mohenjo-daro destroyed

1,000

500 ← Buddha

← Alexander the Great in N. India

Mauryan Empire ← Asoka

0

13 Lost Cities of the Indus

Thousands of years ago the wide plains beside the river Indus were covered with marshland and jungle. Fierce animals roamed freely along its shores. Unhealthy swamps caused disease. But the river itself was full of fish and its valleys were made fertile each year by floods. Despite the dangers, it was understandable that people should settle there. Until recent times little was known about this early Indian civilisation. Within the last forty years, however, the ruins of nearly sixty towns and villages have been found.

Some have hardly been touched. Two in particular, Harappa in the Punjab and Mohenjo-daro in Sind, have been unearthed and studied by archaeologists. Each covers about three square miles and although they are 400 miles apart, both are similar in design. Long, straight streets cross each other at right angles, rather like those of a modern American city. The more important streets are 45 feet wide. Smaller ones were narrow lanes, enclosed by the walls of houses. Many streets had brick drains running down their centre, some with inspection holes. New houses had been built on the ruins of previous dwellings. This was because the river floods rose higher as the years went by and the people tried to live above them. Each city was protected by a fortress built on a man-made hill. In both cases they contained large granaries for storing corn. The one at Harappa, for example, covers 9,000 feet of floor-space.

The Dravidians

Mohenjo-daro and Harappa were not the only discoveries. Other towns have been found at Kalibangan and Chanhu-daro and no doubt there will be more. It seems that at one time, probably between 2500 and 1500 B.C., an area of a thousand square miles, stretching from the Arabian Sea to the Simla Hills, was dotted with the cities and villages of a race which has been named Dravidian. Such people may have wandered originally from East Africa and China during the Stone Ages.

The Dravidians were typical farmers of that time. Fields were terraced for irrigation and earth dams were used to store water or hold the river in check. These were often surprisingly big; one in the Mashkai valley is 348 yards long. The main crops were wheat, barley, peas, melons and possibly dates and cotton. Dogs and cats were kept as pets and cattle and pigs were bred for meat and skins. Camels, asses and horses were available for carrying loads or pulling wooden-wheeled carts.

The long rivers and coastline of this area encouraged trading. Dravidian merchants were in touch with the Mesopotamian empires at certain times. Gold from southern India, copper from Afghanistan and turquoise (blue-green coloured stone) from Iran have been found at Harappa and Mohenjo-daro. Indian pottery has been unearthed in Mesopotamia. This pottery was made on a wheel. It is a pinkish colour with black patterns but sometimes there are pictures of peacocks or fish on the sides. Small statues of kings and goddesses often have heads similar to those found in Mesopotamia so perhaps the Indians were copying the craftsmen of those parts. Bronze or copper objects are rare because this metal had to be imported to the Indus region.

street in the ruined city Mohenjo-daro

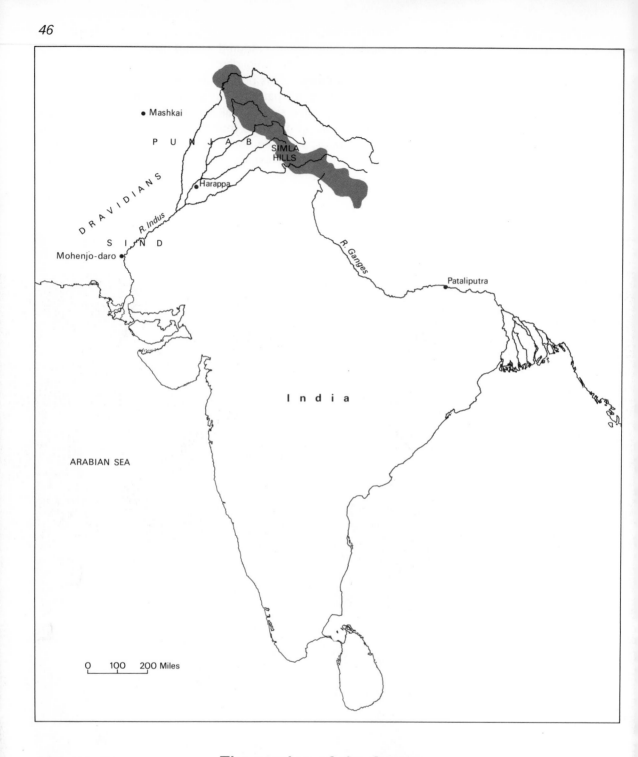

Map labels: Mashkai · , P U N J A B, D R A V I D I A N S, SIMLA HILLS, Harappa · , S I N D, R. Indus, R. Ganges, Mohenjo-daro · , Pataliputra · , I n d i a, ARABIAN SEA, 0 100 200 Miles

Ancient India

The coming of the Aryans

Certain puzzles remain unsolved. Harappa and Mohenjo-daro stand in empty treeless plains. Yet a huge amount of timber was burnt to make the millions of bricks needed to build them. Rain must have been more plentiful than now or few people would have settled there. Perhaps the climate has changed slightly since those times.

Perhaps man himself has changed it by destroying the forests.

The greatest mystery is how this civilisation ended. In about 1500 B.C. people called Aryans (or Indo-Europeans) arrived from Asia. Possibly they fought and defeated the Dravidians who had no iron weapons and were poorly armed. Skeletons have been found lying in disordered heaps in Harappa and Mohenjo-daro. Obviously they were massacred and left unburied. The Aryan hymns to their gods tell of the capture of 'forts' defended by the natives. Such tales could refer to fortress-mounds like those at Harappa and Mohenjo-daro. Apart from wars, it seems likely that disastrous floods caused many inhabitants to leave. The Aryans may have captured mere 'ghost towns' inhabited by a few survivors.

Skeletons found in a house at Mohenjo-daro. In this picture you can see the remains just as the archaeologists found them

14 Indian Religion

Many Aryans settled in the Ganges Valley where their language, religion and way of life have survived until the present-day. Their language was Sanskrit, which is still studied by scholars, though it is only spoken by a few. Their religion grew out of hymns sung by holy men called Brahmins. The popular name for their religion is Hinduism and it is still the chief religion of India (not Pakistan).

Hindus believe that each soul goes through a number of rebirths (re-incarnations). Rebirth into this world of sorrow and pain is thought to be bad, so good deeds reduce the number of rebirths and bad deeds increase them. Throughout the ages India's holy men have argued about what are good or bad deeds. Some have thought that more religious knowledge and deeper faith were good; others that kind and charitable deeds were more important. All have taught that unselfishness is necessary if a soul is to be 'liberated' from rebirth.

Good deeds not only affected the number of times a man was reborn but also his position. Those who had been good were born into four privileged classes or *castes*. Most saintly were the Brahmins who alone could teach the hymns. Next came the Ksatriyas (warrior) caste who were thought fit to rule. Most Indian kings and governors were of this caste. Finally came the Vaisyas who could be merchants, peasants or farmers and the Sudras who were supposed to be servants. All other Hindus were of no class at all. Usually they did rough work or took up trades forbidden to other castes. For example, no caste person was allowed to kill animals so they could not be hunters or butchers. The lowest people of all were the Candalas who were forced to live in special quarters, wear clothes stripped from corpses and eat from cracked bowls and dishes. Such out-castes (untouchables) were believed to have been criminals in a past life. No one was supposed to look at them and they struck pieces of wood to warn others they were coming.

The caste system seems very cruel to us. In fact marriages did take place between persons of different castes and some low caste men did become rich and famous. In any case some holy men disagreed with it. The most famous of these was Gautama, the founder of Buddhism.

The Buddha

Prince Gautama was born in about 500 B.C., the son of an Indian king. Many legends grew up about him. When he was presented at the temple as a baby it was predicted by a wise man that he would one day refuse to be a prince and become a monk when he saw an old man, a sick man and a corpse. His father was worried by this strange prophecy and decided to shut the boy off from such unpleasantness. Gautama lived in a large palace where no servant was allowed to mention illness or death. He was encouraged to marry a beautiful

These golden figures of Buddha are in the Chapel of the Emerald Buddha in Thailand

princess called Yashodara so that he could live a happy family life forgetful of the outside world. When he went out sick or old people were ordered to keep out of sight. Despite these precautions, Gautama one day saw an old man fall in front of his chariot. 'What is this man?' he asked his driver. 'Prince, this is an old man. This is old age,' was the reply. Later he saw a sick man and finally a corpse.

Such signs worried him deeply. Why did people grow old and die, he wondered? Again, how could they escape from their own selfish personality? There must be an answer. He decided to live like a monk, begging for food and owning nothing. At thirty years of age he said goodbye to his wife and little boy and began to wander around India in search of the truth. He listened to what the wisest

Brahmins had to say but still he was not satisfied. He tried starving himself so that he could forget pleasures and think of god but still no answers came. Eventually he found that regular meals and a simple life enabled him to think more clearly. Seated one day under a tree the solution to life's problems came upon him. He became the Buddha, or Enlightened One.

Gautama believed in re-incarnation. But he disagreed with other holy men as to how rebirth could be avoided. To him it seemed that men were reborn because they were always wanting things. If they could only give up these desires they would cease to be reborn and disappear 'like a drop of water in the sea' of Brahma, the great spirit. This blessed state he called Nirvana and he suggested eight ways, the Eightfold Path, which would lead to the end of all desires. Chief among these were right living, right thinking and right doing.

The Buddha taught for over forty years before dying at Oudh. His wife took up his way of life and so did many others. Buddhism was a simple and peaceful belief. It told men to be satisfied with very little and to help and love others. After Gautama's death it continued to spread, especially during the reign of King Asoka (274–236 B.C.).

Siva, a Hindu god

15 The Mauryan Empire

King Asoka began as a conqueror. During one invasion his army slaughtered hundreds of thousands of his enemies. Then the sight of the tortured bodies and the screams of the dying caused him to change. He felt ashamed of his cruelty and soon afterwards became a Buddhist. Instead of going to war he went on pilgrimages. Instead of having several hundred thousand animals killed each day for his kitchens, he reduced the amount to two peacocks and one gazelle. Finally he became a vegetarian.

He also became a much more kind and just ruler. Roads were built all over north western India. Laws were fair and they had to be obeyed. Buddhist missionaries were sent to Persia, Ceylon and Kashmir. When he died this great king had helped to spread the teachings of a man who refused to become a king. Today few Indians are Buddhist but the faith is strong in many parts of the Far East, particularly Burma and Tibet.

Asoka reigned over a large complicated civilisation called the Mauryan empire. (Maurya was the name of the royal family.) It was centred in the valley of the River Ganges but its rule extended both north and south. In previous centuries northern India had been invaded by both Persians and Greeks. These intruders had left but there was plenty to remind Indians of their existence. A great trading road connected Persia and India through Afghanistan. Indian artists and architects copied Persian methods and designs. Chandragupta, Asoka's grandfather, built a great hall at his splendid capital city of Pataliputra which resembled the Persian king's palace at Persepolis. Its many pillars were highly polished and bell-shaped at the top in the Persian manner. A similar column with lion carvings on top belonged to Asoka. It was found at Sarnath and is now the badge of the modern Indian republic.

Trade and farming

In many ways this was the largest and best organised empire in India's history. Well built roads connected the towns and trade was carried on with many far-away countries. Copper and tin came from the Baltic, emeralds and glassware from Egypt, wine from Italy, and silk, saddles and cooking pots from China. India itself sent ivory, precious woods, perfume, pearls, diamonds and rare animals abroad. To exchange these goods, large fleets sailed through shark-filled seas and braved severe storms. By land, caravans of carts and wagons crossed deserts where a pilot had to navigate by the stars as if he were at sea.

Like all ancient civilisations, the root of Mauryan prosperity was farming, particularly rice and sugar growing and cattle breeding. Indian fields were divided into several parts, separated by little embankments and narrow water channels. As the Buddha once put it, they were like a monk's patched cloak. Cattle were so valuable that a man's wealth was measured by how many he owned. Such beasts were used for food, milk, skins, horn and hair. Peasants were the backbone of the empire's wealth, paying a quarter of their crops in government tax.

Like an Egyptian pharaoh, the king was thought of as a god. Each year he ploughed the first furrow personally and if crops were poor it was blamed on his bad rule. He also judged and punished his subjects, using seven thousand books of law as his guide. Trials were long and complicated. Punishments varied from being fined so many heads of cattle to being trampled to death by elephants or thrown head first over a cliff. Prisons were grim places to which the criminal's entire family was sent as well.

Such cruelty is now unknown in India but in many other ways Indian life has not changed much since those far off times.

Asoka's column

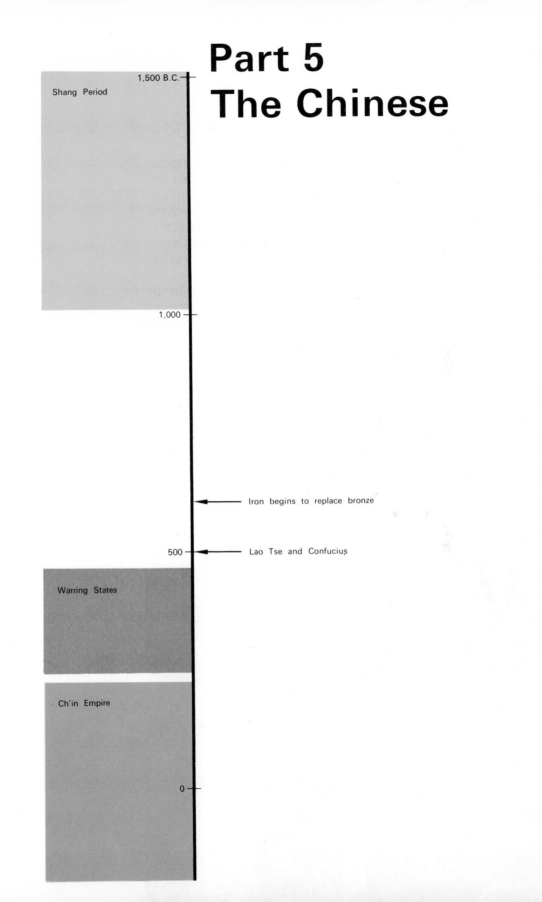

Part 5
The Chinese

Shang Period

1,500 B.C.

1,000

Iron begins to replace bronze

500 — Lao Tse and Confucius

Warring States

Ch'in Empire

0

16 The Land of Three Rivers

Chinese civilisation began in three valleys, those of the Yellow, Yangtze and Huai rivers. Along their banks farmers grew wheat and rice. Such crops needed large amounts of water, particularly rice which grows in flooded fields. The Chinese learnt how to control the rise and fall of such mighty waterways. By 1000 B.C. at the latest they had irrigated the land so successfully that it was able to support a very large population. Further away from these valleys men bred cattle, horses and sheep on land unsuitable for farming.

Ancient China was cut off from other parts of the world. To the south-east was the Pacific Ocean, disturbed by violent typhoons for many months of the year. To the south-west lay the Tibetan plateau and the Himalaya mountains. Only the deserts and mountains of the north offered a possible way into the country for large numbers of intruders. As a result of these barriers the Chinese mixed far less with other races than, for example, the Mediterranean tribes did. Few invaders came and those that did were soon cut off in a similar way and so copied Chinese customs.

Like Egypt, the periods of Chinese history are named after particular families of kings (dynasties). Some of the earliest rulers are known as the Shang (or Yin) kings. Buildings, tombs, bronze pots and treasure pits dating from 1500–1000 B.C. have been found near An-Yang in Honan province. They reveal signs of a people who were skilled in bronze work, who had armies using chariots

Remains of a king's chariot

and kept fowls, pigs, dogs and even elephants as pets. They also scratched signs on bones and gave them to their priests as a way of asking the gods questions. These scratchings are the first signs of what later became the Chinese language.

Shih Huang Ti

It took a long time for the peoples of such a vast region to form one country. At first various large cities merely controlled the country-side and villages around them. Then a few of the more powerful ones conquered their neighbours until there were only seven kingdoms, named Ch'i, Ch'in, Ch'u, Han, Wei, Chao and Yen.

Ancient China

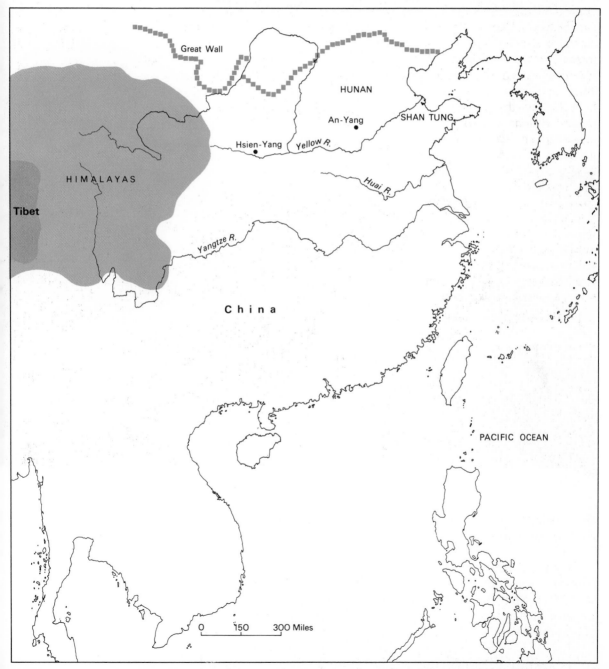

Eventually, Ch'in, whose army was best because it was always fighting the Huns on its borders, overran the other states in 221 B.C.

Its warrior leader called himself Shih Huang Ti (First Universal Emperor) and founded a Ch'in or Chinese empire which lasted until 1911. Shih Huang Ti wanted to give the country a new start. He gave each peasant the land he worked, melted down the weapons of his enemies and ruthlessly destroyed any books he did not approve of. Every time he defeated a rival prince he had an exact copy of his palace built in China's capital, Hsien-Yang. Before he died there were said to be 270 of these palaces.

The separate Chinese states had often built earth walls to keep out invaders from central Asia. Shih Huang Ti and those who ruled after him, the Han emperors, joined these together and strengthened the earth mounds with stone. The resulting Great Wall is 22 feet high, 20 feet wide and runs for 1800 miles. Every hundred yards towers were built to house four or five soldiers. It was never completely successful as a barrier but to this day it remains the largest structure ever created by men.

The Chinese created an unusual civilisation. Their language is difficult to learn because each word is represented by a different sign. It is written downwards instead of across the page. At first the Chinese wrote on bone, strips of bamboo or silk. By A.D. 100 (A.D. stands for Anno Domini, meaning 'In the year of the Lord') they had found a way of turning tree-bark into a paste and spreading it out thinly to dry. In this manner they produced the world's first paper. Chinese craftsmen carved animals and dragons, often from a green stone called jade. Chinese artists were particularly fond of drawing landscapes in black ink on pots, paper, silk and walls. They also like drawings of demons, dragons and spirits.

Rice farming

The Chinese were the first to do many things. As well as inventing the wheelbarrow, they found a way of printing with ink-covered blocks at least eight hundred years before men in the West. They also used gunpowder long before European soldiers. In A.D. 1090 Su-Sung, a government official, even built a huge and complicated clock set in a tower 30 feet high.

But it was as farmers that most Chinese earned a living. A peasant's life was hard. China's climate is unreliable and often a crop is ruined by drought. Rice growing in particular is a difficult job, involving standing in water for hours. Weeds spring up quickly and these have to be cut away. Occasionally there are so many weeds that the rice shoots have to be dug up and replanted elsewhere. An ancient Chinese book on farming gives this advice: 'When the shoots are seven or eight inches long the old weeds will have sprung up again. You must plunge your scythe into the water and hack them at the root; then they will all rot and die.' Such back-breaking work must have become a little easier after iron replaced bronze in about 600 B.C. Then the scythes would have been stronger and sharper.

The Chinese had more than their share of natural disasters. The Yellow River sometimes changed its course as it neared the sea. When this happened acres of fertile farmland and many villages and towns were flooded. Often thousands of people were drowned and those who survived starved to death through lack of food. At times even a good harvest was not sufficient to feed a huge population, for it seems that cities of a million or more inhabitants existed by A.D. 100. Despite the large populations, disease was also widespread.

The Great Wall of China. You can see how vast it is from the size of the people on it

17 Lao Tse and Confucius

Confucius

The ancient Chinese believed that tree and mountain spirits directed all natural forces, such as the sea, wind and rivers. In their view Shang-Ti was the chief god and father of all things whilst the earth was the mother. They also worshipped dead members of their families whose spirits were thought to watch over them. The most powerful spirits were those of the dead emperors.

Everything that happened, good or bad, was thought to be caused by the gods being angry or pleased. On one occasion, for example, it was decided that a drought was being caused by too many prisoners awaiting trial so some were released. When an eclipse of the sun took place one of the early emperors sent for his wise men to find out what he had done wrong. The defeat of a king in battle and the start of a new family of kings was always said to be because the gods had changed their minds about who should rule China. Less powerful than the gods but very troublesome were demons and other evil spirits. Sometimes the doors of the emperor's palace were shut for days to keep them out.

Two great teachers have influenced Chinese life, Lao Tse and Fu-Tzu (Confucius) who both lived about 500 B.C. Lao Tse was the first and he is known as the 'Old Philosopher'. He believed that men should not desire anything, not even goodness. Hatred, greed, pride, ambition were all a waste of time. Rather, men should copy nature. A tree does not want things, or struggle to control other trees. It just grows.

This way of life, called *Tao* from the word for a way or path, took as its motto, 'Leave alone'. It encouraged men to lead simple lives in villages and taught them to love trees, forests and countryside. Some of the greatest Chinese artists have been Taoists, spending their lives drawing the Chinese scenery. Lao Tse was so famous for his wisdom that legends developed around his life. He was said to have been born eighty-one years old. This was a compliment because the ancient Chinese honoured old people.

The Golden Rule

Confucius's teaching was different. Born in Lin Province in 551 B.C., he was horrified by the constant wars between the Chinese kingdoms. When over fifty years old he became Minister of Works and Crimes in Shantung Province. Confucius was convinced that all people could learn to be good simply by following strict rules of behaviour. In his opinion, obedience to one's elders, consideration for others, kindness and politeness could be learnt. A start would be made if everyone followed his Golden Rule, 'Never do to other people what you do not want them to do to you'.

Teaching could be done either by advice or by example. In

particular, a king or emperor must set a good example to his subjects. Only then would he be worthy to rule. The ignorant people must, in turn, obey their leaders who cared so much for them. In Shantung Confucius himself showed the way. He carefully selected the most suitable men for each job, punished criminals fairly and saw that all workmen were well fed. Soon there were hardly any prisoners to go to gaol.

Confucius was not a religious leader. He did not teach people about god or life after death. 'How can we know about death when we have learnt so little about life?' he once asked. His aim was to show men how to behave properly and so to improve their characters. For example, he said a boy must always call his father 'honourable' and refer to himself as an 'unworthy son'. A subject must not just bow before his king but touch the ground with his forehead in what is called kow-tow. Soldiers were to be despised because of their violent ways. Scholars were to be admired because of their knowledge and good manners. Confucius wrote down old tales and poems but altered them so that they contained a useful lesson, or moral. This book, *Spring and Autumn Annals,* was given to his first followers with the remark, 'By these I shall be known and by these I shall be judged'.

Picture by a Taoist artist. It shows a demon-killer on his travels

Unfortunately, later generations of priests and scholars altered the teachings of both Lao Tse and Confucius. Magical ceremonies were introduced into Taoist living. Temples were built where

Confucianism could be studied even though it was not a religion. People were still told that they must obey the emperor, but emperors were no longer expected to set a good example, or to make their subjects happy. Confucian ceremonies were strictly carried out even though their purpose, to make men good, was often ignored.

When China became an empire her rulers found they needed a large number of officials (mandarins) to help them govern. To become a mandarin difficult tests were set. Each year thousands of candidates would take food, candles and writing equipment into special little cells and struggle for days and nights to answer difficult questions about the writings of Confucius and other scholars. Only a few passed. Yet a mandarin's job was such a pleasant one that many officials were merely chosen by their relatives or friends. Some men bought a post with bribes, or were picked because they or their families were known to the emperor.

None of this would have pleased Lao Tse or Confucius. But the 'Old Philosopher' would probably have blamed Confucius for the trouble. He could never understand why Confucius worried so much about changing people and ordering their lives. Legend tells how the two met and Lao Tse said, 'Wherefore this undue energy? The swan is white without a daily bath; the raven is black without daily colouring itself'. Nevertheless, both Taoism and Confucianism have greatly influenced Chinese life through the ages.

Cells where future mandarins took their examinations

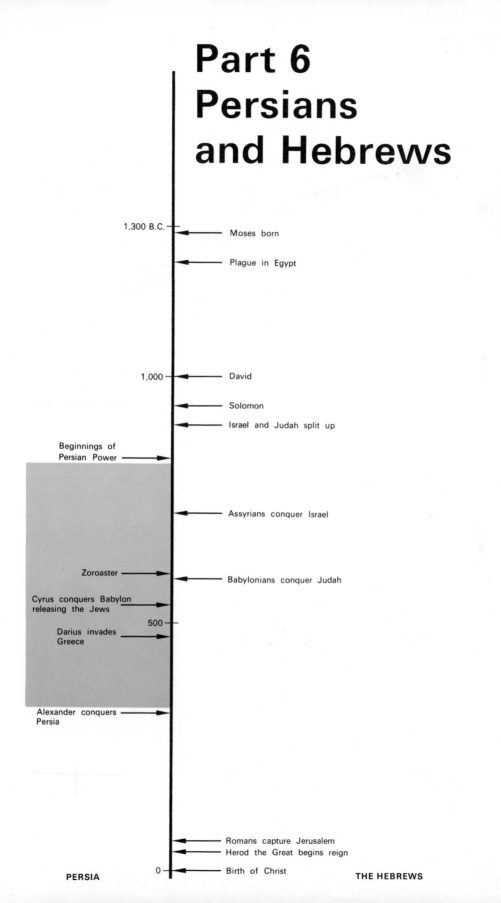

Part 6
Persians
and Hebrews

1,300 B.C. — ← Moses born

← Plague in Egypt

1,000 — ← David

← Solomon

← Israel and Judah split up

Beginnings of
Persian Power ——→

← Assyrians conquer Israel

Zoroaster ——→ ← Babylonians conquer Judah

Cyrus conquers Babylon
releasing the Jews ——→

500 —
Darius invades ——→
Greece

Alexander conquers ——→
Persia

← Romans capture Jerusalem
← Herod the Great begins reign
0 — ← Birth of Christ

PERSIA   **THE HEBREWS**

18 The Persians

Although the Iranian plateau is often called Persia, most of its ancient tribes were Medes. The true Persians had arrived from central Asia in about 900 B.C. They conquered the Aryans on the edge of the Iranian desert and by 836 B.C. were important enough to have a separate king. Eventually, they settled in the province of Fars, a remote spot ringed with mountains and desert and therefore easy to defend against the slow, heavily equipped Assyrians. As a result, this small tribe of horsebreeders and farmers remained safe whilst others were conquered. Their new home gave them another advantage because the wind-swept hills of Fars are more healthy than the plains of the Persian Gulf.

The most famous Persian king, Cyrus the Great, once remarked, 'Soft countries breed soft men. You will never find in one soil luxurious fruits and fine soldiers too.' This was certainly true of his own people. When they took to farming they overcame many difficulties. We can still see the stone channels which they built to carry water miles up into the mountains. When they followed Cyrus to war they quickly conquered an empire he called proudly, 'the Kingdom of the Whole World'.

The Persian Empire

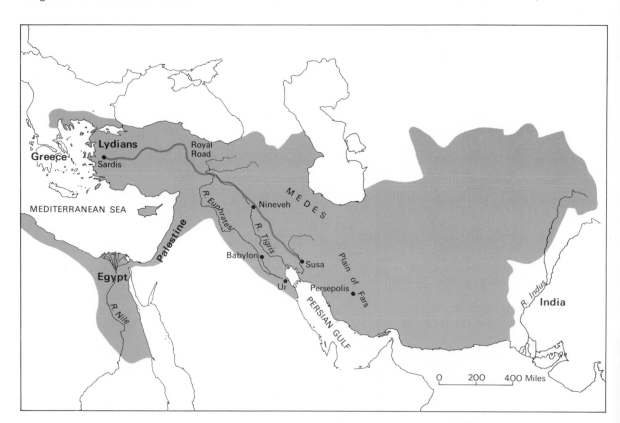

From Egypt to the borders of India, his enemies collapsed before the arrows of his bowmen and the charge of his cavalry. Yet the Persians never forgot who they were or where they came from. In later years many races lived under Persian rule and many men marched in its armies. But only Persians held important government posts, only Persians were freed from paying taxes, and only Persians were recruited for the Empire's finest troops, the Immortals, who wore gold embroidered gowns and carried spears decorated with silver.

'The Empire of the whole world'

Cyrus defeated the Medes, then the Lydians and finally the Babylonians before he was killed in battle. His son, Cambyses, conquered Egypt. After Cambyses's death there were revolts but these were crushed by Darius who reigned at the time of Persia's greatest power. Unlike the Assyrians, the Persians were good rulers who allowed subject races to live in their own way, without interference.

Each of the twenty provinces of the empire was controlled by a *satrap* (governor). To make sure the satraps did their jobs properly spies moved about the empire reporting on them to the king. These 'Ears of the King' were not popular and they had to be guarded by soldiers. Nevertheless, they helped to turn the Great King's land into one of the best governed empires of ancient times.

Many good roads were built to bind this vast area together. The 'Royal Road' from Susa to Sardis, for example, was 1,600 miles long. Every fourteen miles there were rest stations where a messenger could change horses. A royal order could be sent the length of the road in a week. The Persians also developed silver mines, repaired the old canal used by Hatshepsut's ships and built large temples which resembled Babylonian and Assyrian buildings. Their scholars used an alphabet of thirty-nine letters. They were interested in astronomy and learnt a great deal from the Babylonians on this subject.

Zoroaster

The Persians followed the teachings of Zoroaster, who lived in about 600 B.C. Little is certain about him. He is said to have dwelt alone for fifteen years, to have been carried up to heaven at various times and to have taught for ten years without converting anyone. What is clear is that he preached a new version of an old religion which may have been connected with Hinduism.

Zoroaster claimed that life was a fight between good and evil. On one side there was Ahriman (Destructive Spirit), the god of darkness and evil; on the other Ahuramazda (Wise Lord), the god of light and truth who struggled to defeat him. In one of his hymns he explains it like this: 'Now the two primal spirits, who revealed themselves in visions as Twins, are the Better and the Bad in thought and word and action.'

To help Ahuramazda in his fight with Ahriman, a Zoroastrian had to live a good life. He must be honest, truthful and polite and a friend to both people and animals. As a guide he had a set of poems written by Zoroaster which were usually printed in gold letters on

Persian archers on a decorated brick wall

animal skins. When a true Zoroastrian died he passed through fire without being hurt and, for him, the bridge leading from earth to heaven was wide. A bad man, however, would find the bridge so narrow that he would fall off and never reach paradise.

Much of the consideration and kindness with which the Persians ruled their empire was the result of following Zoroaster. Most of the famous Persian kings were Zoroastrians. On one inscription, Darius proclaimed: 'Such was Ahuramazda's will, he chose me a man, out of the whole earth and made me king of the whole earth.' Another king, Ataxerxes I, introduced a new calendar with all the months named after Zoroastrian gods. All conquered people were well treated and even the Greeks, their enemies, admitted that to a Persian truth was a great virtue and to tell a lie a most dreadful crime.

In later times the Romans copied some of Zoroaster's beliefs in their worship of the god, Mithras. The Muslims, on the other hand, conquered Persia in the seventh century A.D. and ruthlessly wiped out this gentle religion. Today a mere 125,000 Zoroastrians survive. Some still live in Persia. Others, called Parsees, are in India. But when Cyrus ruled his 'Kingdom of the Whole World' he spread the religion far and wide. In Babylon it was studied by the Jews he released from slavery (see Chapter 20). In this way the belief in a battle between good and evil and in judgment after death entered Jewish religion and so Christianity.

The ruins of the palace of Persepolis

19 God's Chosen People

The Hebrews were a small tribe of shepherds and cattle-breeders. They seem to have settled first at Ur until they were driven away by Hammurabi. From Ur they moved to Haran and finally wandered south under their leader Abraham. According to the Bible, even at this early stage they had received a promise from God. One day, Abraham was told, the Jews would inhabit the land of Canaan (see map), and become a great nation.

This promise made the Jews different from other peoples. Most ancient tribes worshipped cruel and sometimes wicked gods who were thought to need blood sacrifices. Only the Jews believed in a god who had given them a special task to do. To them, God was so sacred that they never spoke his name. His initials were YHWH and to us he is known as Jehovah. It was Jehovah who, according to the Bible, said to the Jews: 'I will put my law in their inward parts, and in their hearts will I write it; and I will be their God, and they shall be my people.'

After many years these desert wanderers found themselves in

Israel and Judah

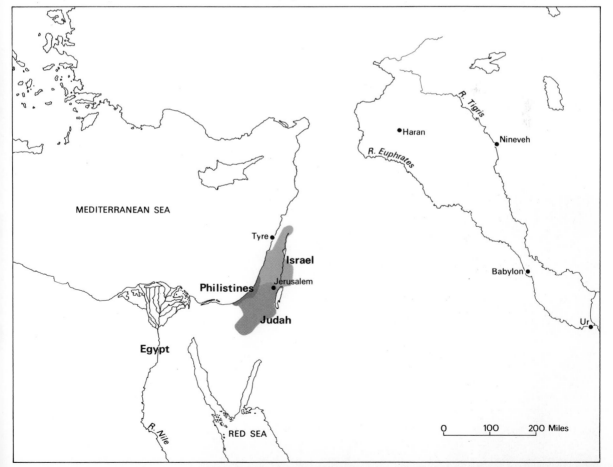

Egypt at the time of the Hyksos pharaohs (see Chapter 12). The Bible stories show clearly that they were welcome. Unfortunately, when the Hyksos were driven out, the Egyptians turned their hatred on the Jews as well. From being favoured friends of the government, they became little more than slaves. They were given exhausting work to do and were cruelly punished if they slacked or grumbled. Sometimes even their children were killed. It seemed that Jehovah had forgotten his people.

Moses

The Jews were saved by a great leader, Moses. He was born in Egypt about 1305 B.C. and found by the pharaoh's daughter, Bithya, abandoned in some bullrushes by the river. The name Moses means in Hebrew, 'I have rescued him from the water'. Bithya had him brought up as an Egyptian nobleman. He wore fine clothes, learnt Egyptian ways and went on military expeditions with the pharaoh's army.

One day this strong, quick-tempered man saw an Egyptian beating a Jewish slave. He remembered that he was a Jew also and he struck the Egyptian so hard that he killed him. Horrified, he buried the body but soon afterwards a chance remark showed that his action was known to others. To save himself, Moses left the easy, pleasant life of the Egyptian court and went to live with a desert tribe, the Midianites. In such simple, peaceful surroundings he had time to think.

One day, we are told, Jehovah spoke to him from a burning bush, telling him that he must lead the Jews out of Egypt. Immediately he returned to the country where he had committed a murder. At first the pharaoh merely laughed at Moses's warnings and demands. His god was not the god of the Jews. Anyway, the Jews were doing much useful work. They could not be spared. But as a series of plagues and other disasters started to torment Egypt, the pharaoh began to wonder if this was the work of the Jewish god. Blood, frogs,

Mt. Sinai

flies, wild beasts, disease, boils, hailstones, locusts and darkness were said to have troubled the unfortunate Egyptians.

At last, in about 1230 B.C., the pharaoh agreed to let them go. Even as he did so, the Bible tells how the worst disaster of all, the death of all first-born children, came upon Egypt. To the sound of crying and moaning, the Jews left the country which had been their prison for so many years. And when a revengeful Egyptian army chased after them it was drowned in the Red Sea.

God's laws

This movement out of Egypt—the Exodus as it is called—was the most important event in Jewish history because Moses proved to be a great law-giver as well as a successful leader. On Mount Sinai, God gave him those Ten Commandments which have been an essential part of Jewish religion ever since.

Thou shalt have no other gods before me.

Thou shalt not make unto thee any graven image [statue]. Thou shalt not bow down thyself to them, nor serve them.

Thou shalt not take the name of the Lord thy God in vain.

Remember the Sabbath day to keep it holy.

Honour thy father and thy mother.

Thou shalt not kill.

Thou shalt not commit adultery.

Thou shalt not steal.

Thou shalt not bear false witness[tell lies] against thy neighbour.

Thou shalt not covet [want] thy neighbour's house, nor wife, nor maidservant.

Part of an early version of the Book of Isaiah, from a Jewish scroll found near the Dead Sea

Later he received 613 commands which when written down amounted to 5,845 verses. These laws are called by Jews the *Torah*, meaning 'The Way'.

The Torah represents a new kind of religion. Previous peoples had never thought of their gods as being good, or as wanting human beings to be good. In the Torah, for the first time, God was described as a lover of goodness. The Jewish God is a God of truth and love. His laws are far different from those of Marduk or other ancient gods. Instead of 'an eye for an eye and a tooth for a tooth', he commands, 'Thou shalt not take vengeance, nor bear any grudge against the children of the people, but thou shalt love thy neighbour as thyself'. Instead of human and animal sacrifices he demands only that a person should live a good life. Instead of only working mysterious miracles through special priests, we read in the Bible, 'And the Lord spoke unto Moses face to face, as a man speaketh unto his friend'.

Of course, not all the laws were as important as the Ten Commandments. Moses was faced with the problem of keeping an unruly people united in wild surroundings. Many laws deal with how the nightly camp should be set up or how fires and cooking should be organised. In particular, eating was strictly controlled. Only cattle with divided hoofs—oxen, sheep, goats—and fish with fins and scales were to be eaten. The pig, which is usually dirtier, could not be eaten. Such laws may seem strange to us but they were no doubt necessary when food was not as carefully cleaned as it is today.

20 Baal and Jehovah

Moses died before his people reached 'the promised land'. The next leader, Joshua, was more warlike and under him the Jews began the conquest of Canaan. It took many years because a fierce tribe, the Philistines, lived in the best parts of the country. Only slowly did the Jews fight their way out of the mountains, forests and wilderness and take over the more fertile farmlands of the south. It was 1000 B.C. before a united Jewish state was founded under King David with its capital in the ancient city of Jerusalem. This was a great day for the descendants of Abraham. Joyously, the tribesmen called their new country 'Israel' which means 'God strives'. This was probably an old battle cry.

Unfortunately their troubles were far from over. The new kingdom was small, sandwiched between the strong states of Egypt and Mesopotamia. For some years it managed to survive through the temporary weakness of Egypt and its own alliance with the prosperous Phoenician city of Tyre. The king of Tyre wished to secure a trade route through the Israelite hills to the Red Sea. This desire made him friendly and helpful.

The kingdom became rich for a time. Jerusalem was enlarged and fortified with a city wall. Its most prosperous king, Solomon, built a magnificent temple and a royal palace. In later years, however, the powerful Mesopotamian city states of Assyria and Babylon arose to menace God's 'Chosen People'.

The Babylonian captivity

After King Solomon's death a quarrel split the country in two, with Israel to the north and a separate state called Judah to the south. Both were conquered. In 722 B.C. the Assyrians occupied Israel and killed or enslaved many of its people. They allowed their own countrymen to take over farms in the area. These colonists settled down and were known as Samaritans. Two centuries later a Babylonian army overran Judah, sending even more Jews into slavery. This 'Babylonian captivity' lasted for about sixty years. During that time the first books of the Bible were written. It ended when the Persian king, Cyrus, set the Jews free after his capture of Babylon in 538 B.C.

Various religious leaders, called prophets, tried to explain these defeats. The Jews, they said, had been punished for disobeying God's laws. If only they would return to the ways of Moses their enemies would be struck down just as the plagues had punished Egypt. Amos, Hosea and Isaiah said this when the Assyrians were coming. As the Babylonian armies closed in, the Lord told another prophet, Jeremiah: 'Because ye have not heard my words, behold I will send the King of Babylon against this land, and against the inhabitants thereof, and against all these nations round about, and will utterly destroy them.'

King Solomon, reading *The Torah*

The Wailing Wall in Jerusalem, built on the site of Solomon's temple. The Wall is all that is left of a later temple destroyed by the Romans

Such punishments seemed just because, in fact, many Israelites had broken their promise to God. When they had entered Canaan years before the Jews had found a nature religion far different from their own beliefs. We know a great deal about it because of descriptions found on clay tablets in Syria. The Canaanites' chief god was Baal who was 'Lord of the Earth' and whose voice was heard in the thunder. Each year he died at harvest time and was reborn in the spring. Without his help it was thought that drought and disease would ruin the farmers' crops. For this reason each village had an open-air holy place where the god was offered burnt animals and sometimes children. Sacrifices were performed on a stone slab called an altar; the word means 'the place where the slaughtering is done'. Around these places priests conducted musical and dancing ceremonies.

From the start the Jews had wondered whether Jehovah, the god of deserts and shepherds, would be able to make crops grow. Many decided to worship both Baal and Jehovah and as time went on the muddle grew worse. Creatures honoured by the Canaanites, such as the snake and bull, were worshipped as forms of Jehovah on earth. The annual harvest feast of Canaan was combined with the Jewish Passover feast, held to celebrate the escape from Egypt. Canaanite religious ceremonies and even the Canaanite language were taken over by the Jews. The famous Temple built by King Solomon shows clearly how the two religions had been mixed up. At the entrance stood an altar for burnt offerings. Yet inside was a holy place where the laws of Moses were kept carved on stone tablets.

Help from heaven

Not all Jews disobeyed their God. In desert areas tribes, such as the Rechabites and Nazirites, still despised the 'farmers' god'. They lived only in skin and hair cloth tents, because weaving was a farmers' habit, refused to drink wine because the vine does not grow in the desert and never cut their hair because there had been no razors during the Exodus.

It was from such tribes that there came the prophets who obeyed the teachings of Jehovah. Repeatedly Amos, Hosea, Isaiah, Jeremiah and others called upon the people to give up Canaanite ways and return to the worship of the one true God. Again and again they predicted disaster if the Jews did not. Generally they were proved right as one conquest followed another. Eventually the unfortunate Jews forgot about winning battles by ordinary means. Instead they turned more and more to the hope that a God-sent 'Saviour' would come and rescue them.

In a way they were right. No earthly power could bring them military victory against the Assyrians and the Babylonians. On the other hand, because enough Jews still believed in the simple faith taught by Moses, they were able to keep alight a religious spark which burst into flame as Christianity. As a result a small tribe one day changed world history.

Part 7
The Greek World

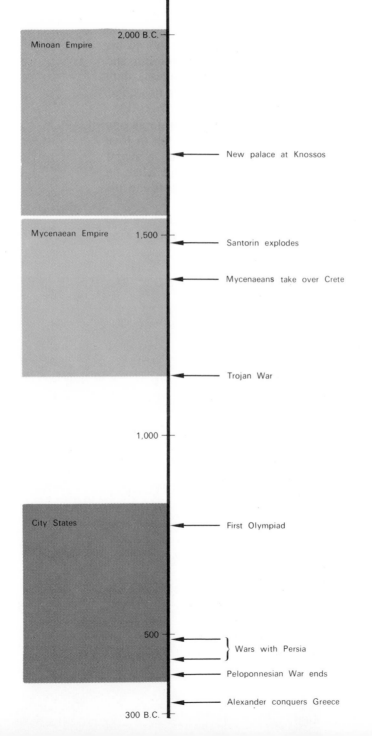

Minoan Empire

2,000 B.C.

New palace at Knossos

Mycenaean Empire   1,500 — Santorin explodes

Mycenaeans take over Crete

Trojan War

1,000

City States

First Olympiad

500

} Wars with Persia

Peloponnesian War ends

Alexander conquers Greece

300 B.C.

21 Minoan Crete

The Greeks used to tell a strange tale about the narrow, mountainous island of Crete. Long ago the king of Athens had killed the son of King Minos of Crete. In revenge, Minos conquered Athens and ordered seven young men and seven young girls to be sent to his island each year. These prisoners were driven one by one into the labyrinth, a maze of tunnels where they wandered aimlessly until they were eaten by the *Minotaur*, a monster with a bull's head and the body of a man.

One day Theseus, son of an Athenian king, offered to go as one of the fourteen. The Cretan king's daughter, Ariadne, fell in love with him. Before he entered the labyrinth she gave him a sword and some string. Theseus laid the thread behind him and when he met the Minotaur he killed it with the sword. Then he found his way out by following the trail of string.

Triumphantly, he sailed back to Greece but forgot that he had promised to hoist white sails if successful. When his father, King

This wall painting shows the sport of bull-leaping, which may have suggested the Minotaur story. The man in the picture (coloured red) is about to be caught by the woman (coloured white) behind the bull

Aegeus, saw black sails instead of white he thought his son was dead. Overcome with grief, he threw himself into the sea and was drowned. For this reason it is known as the Aegean Sea.

Painting of a Cretan lady

The Palace of Knossos

It sounded little more than a legend until Sir Arthur Evans, an archaeologist, arrived in Crete in 1894 to find that ancient walls had been unearthed from a huge mound at Knossos. He decided to investigate and in 1900 his workmen began to uncover a large palace spread over six acres. Set around a central courtyard 170 feet long and 80 feet wide were many passages and rooms as well as a complicated drainage system.

Some rooms had been used to store grain and oil; others contained precious jewels and one a throne. An outer staircase of brilliant white stone was lined with beautiful and unusual columns which tapered at the bottom. On the walls were brightly coloured paintings showing dark-haired women and athletic men. The women had thick make-up, jewelled combs in their hair, and wore long, graceful gowns. The men dressed in short trousers with feathers on their heads. In some cases men and women were shown somersaulting over bulls in an arena. Obviously a rich and powerful king had once ruled a civilised people. Many ingredients of the old story were at Knossos—the labyrinth, the bulls, the great king.

Minoan life

A great deal of this ancient Cretan world lies buried forever under farmland. Consequently its full story will never be known. But the size of the palace suggests that a population of at least 40,000 once lived at Knossos. Evans's discoveries showed that Crete had been civilised from about 3000 B.C. Because some of its kings were named Minos, he called this civilisation Minoan.

The Minoans seem to have been gay and pleasure loving. Their buildings were often several storeys high with bright coloured bands painted across them. Their religion appears to have been a happy one. No demons, goblins or evil gods decorate the walls of Knossos. An Earth Mother was worshipped in pleasant, woodland shrines, not large temples. She was offered fruit, poppies and perhaps bulls as a sacrifice. Houses seem to have been 'protected' by a snake goddess who was represented in statuettes.

The men of Crete were sailors and fishermen who loved hunting and bull-baiting. They possessed large fleets because they had plenty of wood for shipbuilding and long beaches on which it was

The Early Greek World

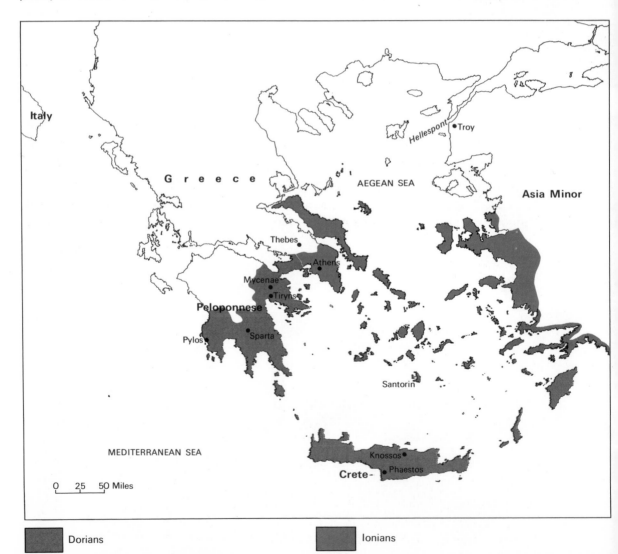

easy to drag a boat ashore. They made a living by trading or piracy. No traces of their ships or dockyards have been discovered but as there are no forts on land it seems they relied mainly on a fleet for defence. Minos was probably a merchant or pirate king, ruling an island which stood conveniently on the ancient trade routes between Egypt, Palestine, Asia Minor and Greece. His people exported wool and timber and brought copper from Cyprus, tin from Greece and luxury goods like precious stones from Egypt.

The Cretans were the first Europeans known to have been civilised. They grew corn and fruit and made articles from gold, silver, copper and tin. Their pots and jugs were decorated with pictures of octopuses, plants, grass and, sometimes, a curling 'S' line. They also made delicate statuettes from ivory or wood. In a sunlit, beautiful land, the Minoans lived a generally peaceful life threatened only by earthquakes. About 1500 B.C. for example, the island of Thera, now called Santorin, sixty miles from Crete, blew up. Enormous waves, travelling at great speed, destroyed many Cretan coastal towns whilst other earth tremors shattered the palace of Knossos.

Evans himself experienced a slight earthquake in 1926. 'A dull sound rose from the ground, like the muffled roar of an angry bull,' he wrote. Perhaps this was the sort of sound which gave rise to the legend of the Minotaur?

Linear A and B

Whilst digging at Knossos, Evans found about three thousand clay tablets with symbols and signs carved on them. There were two different kinds which scholars called Linear A and B. Each was developed from the outlines of an earlier 'picture' writing. Linear A remains a mystery even though examples of it have been found all over Crete. It is probably the language of the ancient Cretans. In 1953 an English architect, Michael Ventris, discovered that Linear B was a shorthand way of writing Greek. This was exciting news because, although 'B' tablets had only been found at Knossos in Crete, they have turned up in Greece at Pylos, Mycenae and Thebes. This was because the earliest known Greeks, called Mycenaeans after their chief city, had conquered Crete in about 1450 B.C.

Mycenaeans entered Greece from the north in about 2000 B.C. Being tough fighting shepherds they easily defeated the Pelasgians already living there. Their conquest of Crete is very important because they copied the ways of this more civilised race. As a result Cretan civilisation entered the mainland of Europe.

A snake-goddess figure made out of ivory and gold

A *linear B* tablet, made of clay baked hard by fire

22 Mycenae and Troy

The chief Mycenaean cities were Mycenae itself, Thebes, Pylos and Tiryns. Here these warriors built large palaces and forts. You can see the great 'Lion Gate' at Mycenae in the photograph. The idea of two animals facing each other is a Cretan one. Some of the stones used by the Mycenaeans were very large, weighing as much as 130 tons. Later people refused to believe these stones could have been moved by ordinary men. Such fortress-palaces seemed the work of giants so they made up tales of a one-eyed giant called Cyclops.

The Mycenaeans loved fighting and hunting wild animals like the wolf and wild boar; they painted their walls with war scenes rather than beautiful ladies. But they did settle down to farming, growing wheat, barley, millet and peas. Vines were cultivated and the wine made from the grapes was sweetened with honey. Their noblemen lived a life similar to knights in the Middle Ages. Castles dotted the countryside, defended by well-armed soldiers with bronze swords and immense 'tower' shields which protected them from head to foot.

When a leader died he was buried in a stone tomb shaped like a beehive. One of the largest at Mycenae is called the Treasury of Atreus after one of their kings. A dead king was buried with his weapons, his gold belt and other equipment. Around him lay precious rings, daggers and necklaces. His face was covered with a gold mask. Rich women dressed in Cretan-style clothes and admired themselves in polished bronze mirrors. Dogs were kept as pets and for hunting.

Homer and Schliemann

The Mycenaeans were keen traders. Their ships voyaged to Syria, Palestine and Egypt. To be a pirate was considered a good thing. In about 1150 B.C. they fought a long war with Troy, a city in Asia Minor (modern Turkey). According to the Greek poet Homer, who lived about 400 years later, this war was caused because Paris, son of Priam, king of Troy, carried off Helen, the beautiful wife of the king of Sparta. More probably the war was caused by a quarrel about trading rights in the narrow strip of water leading from the Mediterranean into the Black Sea. Certainly the Greeks were swarming all over the eastern Mediterranean region at this time, trading and founding settlements or colonies. It was natural that the original inhabitants should resent this.

Homer called the Mycenaeans, Achaeans. His long poem, the *Iliad* (the story of Ilium, another name for Troy) tells how the Achaeans, led by kings like Achilles and Agamemnon, tried for ten years to take the city. Fierce battles in which even the gods were supposed to have taken part led to the death of many heroes. At last the Greeks pretended to sail away but left a large, hollow wooden

The Lion Gate leading into the fortress at Mycenae

horse outside the Trojan walls. Inside it were Greeks under the command of the cunning Odysseus. Full of curiosity, the Trojans broke down a section of their wall to drag the horse within the city.

After dark, Odysseus's men climbed out and attacked the guards. The rest of the Greeks returned and Troy was destroyed.

Like the legend of the Minotaur, it sounds an interesting story but little more. For centuries western readers enjoyed Homer's tales but regarded them as fairy stories. About a hundred years ago, however, a young German, Heinrich Schliemann, decided that they were true. In the evening after he finished work in a grocery shop, he dreamed of finding Troy. To help his search he learnt Greek as well as nine other languages. Later, when he had become rich, he went to Turkey to organise an archaeological expedition. Using Homer's actual words as his guide he made his way to a mound at Hissarlik. Sure enough, his workmen uncovered the remains of nine cities, one on top of the other. The Troy of which Homer wrote stood on top of six earlier ruins.

Afterwards Schliemann led expeditions to Mycenae where he found other extraordinary things. Homer had told how Agamemnon, the Greek leader, had been murdered on his return from the capture of Troy. His body and the bodies of his nobles were supposed to have been buried by the Lion Gate. Schliemann dug near this gate and uncovered six graves containing nineteen bodies. The male skeletons were decorated in the very clothes and armour described by Homer.

Schliemann even thought that one body was Agamemnon himself. Excitedly he gazed upon the face behind the gold mask. After a few seconds it crumbled into dust. We now know it was not the corpse of the old Greek hero but of a soldier who lived 250 years before Agamemnon's time. Even so, Schliemann's work revealed to the world the whole story of Mycenaean Greece.

The mask Schliemann thought belonged to Agamemnon

Dorian invasions

When their power was at its height, the Mycenaeans traded with most Mediterranean countries. Their ships brought goods from Syria, Sicily, Cyprus and perhaps Britain: Stonehenge may have been designed by a Mycenaean architect. But around 1250 B.C. movements of population led to attacks on civilised places by barbarian tribes. In such confused conditions, trading in the eastern Mediterranean became difficult. As trade declined the Mycenaean cities grew poorer. The sort of wealth which had paid for the 'Lion Gate' was no longer available. The city that Homer described as 'rich in gold' shrank until it was little more than a village. When a fierce mountain people, the Dorians, descended from the north armed with iron swords the Mycenaeans were soon beaten.

Dorian tribes settled chiefly in the Peloponnese, an area named after a Mycenaean King Pelops (ruddy face). Later they conquered Crete. The Dorians were a stern, disciplined race who used their subjects as slaves. Many Mycenaeans fled before them and settled in Attica and Asia Minor. These refugees are known as Ionians after the Greek dialect they spoke.

Dorians and Ionians grew to be the two most famous Greek races. The chief Dorian city was Sparta. The most important in Ionia was Athens.

23 Athens and Sparta

Today if you look at a map of the Mediterranean area you will see the boundaries of a country, Greece, with its capital city, Athens. In ancient times, however, most Greek towns were self-governing and there was no state called Greece. Indeed, many famous Greek cities were not on the Greek mainland at all, but in Sicily, Asia Minor and North Africa. Even the word Greece was unknown. The Greeks called themselves Hellenes and their original homeland, Hellas; it was the Romans who called them Greeks. A Greek knew he belonged to a separate race which had settled along parts of the Mediterranean coast. If abroad, he often felt a love for his 'mother city' in Greece. But generally he was loyal only to the *polis* (city state) in which he lived.

Ancient Greece

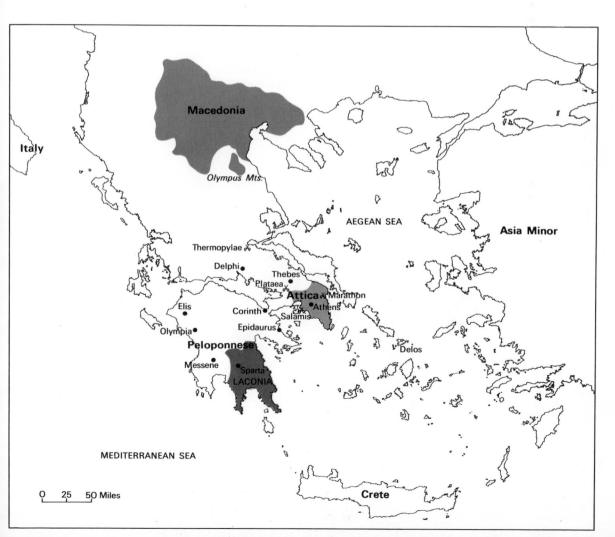

City states

Every polis, and there were a great number of them, was small by modern standards. Only three, Syracuse and Acragas in Sicily and Athens itself, ever had more than 20,000 citizens. This figure does not include women or slaves, as only free men who could vote were called citizens. Most city states were about a quarter of this size and some were tiny. The remains of Mycenae, for example, once sent an 'army' of eighty-four men to a battle.

A polis usually controlled farmland sufficient to feed its people and was near enough to the sea to earn a living by trade or fishing. There was rarely any need for cities to unite permanently and most of the 'leagues' which were formed quickly fell apart. In any case,

the Greeks were quarrelsome folk who disliked taking orders from outsiders.

In early times Greek cities were often ruled by kings. These monarchies were usually followed by the rule of a few rich families (an *oligarchy*). Later, some preferred to govern themselves by electing their leaders (a *democracy*). Few Greek cities allowed every adult to vote as we do today. Nevertheless a Greek citizen could never feel forgotten or ignored. If he was taxed to pay for a wall or a temple he could watch it being built. If he was rich and paid for, say, a warship he might be expected to command it himself. If he wrote a play he nearly always acted in it and sometimes designed the costumes as well. His rulers were known to him personally. If he felt annoyed about some matter he could argue with his representative next time he met him in the street or *agora* (market place).

Even the least free of all Greek cities, Sparta, chose its leaders at a meeting of male citizens over thirty years of age. The most freedom-loving, Athens, insisted that every man go to its Assembly to help govern the state. Each month fifty Athenian councillors from one of ten tribes took turns to run the city's affairs. When the Assembly was in session the streets were empty and voters came by horse or boat from outlying districts. A long rope was swept across the agora. Any Athenian who lingered there and was brushed by it was fined for not being on the Pnyx Hill where the Assembly met!

Ruins of the market place at Athens

Sparta

Most of the interesting and beautiful things about the Greeks—their painting, sculpture, plays, science and philosophy—were at their best in Athens. Its carvings and pottery, its wonderful buildings, its plays and ways of government, are still copied and admired today. Its rival, Sparta, a powerful Greek city which ruled over twenty-four neighbouring towns, was far different. Very few ancient cities even looked like Sparta. If a traveller approached it by day he noticed at once that it had no walls. This was to make its people fight harder when attacked! If he reached it by night no lights were to be seen. This was to make its soldiers skilled at night marching.

The reason for these and other strange customs went back a long way. In early times the Spartans enslaved some of the peoples around them. These *helots*, as they were called, were very badly treated. They were beaten if they did not work hard enough and murdered if they protested. Having decided to live on the labour of others, the Spartans were forced to be soldiers, for only then would they be safe from a helot rebellion. A certain Lycurgus—who may never have existed—is said to have worked out a system of training designed to produce magnificent soldiers.

Selection began at birth. The strong alone survived; weak or deformed babies were left to die on Mount Tygetus or thrown from its steep sides. At seven years of age all boys were taken from their mothers and put in special barracks. Here they learned to cook, sleep on rushes and walk barefoot in winter and summer. They were kept short of food and so forced to steal rations from grown-ups. Boys not caught stealing were admired; those who were discovered were beaten unmercifully.

At twenty, Spartan men went to live in barracks as part of an army club. Meals consisted of barley bread, figs, cheese and a kind of haggis. This haggis was so revolting that after one dinner a foreign visitor remarked, 'Now I understand why Spartans do not fear death'. Even after marriage a Spartiate (trained Spartan soldier) lived permanently in the clubs and only visited his family occasionally.

Kings and ephors

Sparta was ruled by two kings. This unusual arrangement was supposed to have started when a Spartan queen gave birth to twins and refused to say which had been born first. Whether this tale is true or not, the scheme had certain advantages. It prevented one leader from becoming too powerful and meant that in wartime only one need go away to fight. Besides these two, five *ephors* (judges) and and an Assembly of thirty elders *(gerousia)* helped govern the town.

The ephors were particularly powerful. When elected they promised 'to shave off their moustaches and obey the laws' during their year of office. No one could defy their rules, which were enforced without mercy. They could even arrest or fine a king who did wrong. Once they punished a ruler who married a small woman because they said 'she will bear us not kings but kinglets'. Candidates for the gerousia appeared in person before the Assembly. Those who received the loudest cheer were elected. Owing to their hatred of outsiders, there were only a few true Spartans and their numbers grew smaller as time went on.

It was easy to laugh at the Spartans and many Greeks did. In fact there were things to admire in their way of life. They were very loyal to their leaders. When a king died a man and woman from each household deliberately injured themselves, whilst women roamed the streets crying and banging cooking pots. Spartans also respected old people. At one Olympic Games an elderly man was unable to find a chair because of the crowds. Everyone ignored him until he reached the Spartan section. Then every man rose and offered him a seat. Thankfully he murmured, 'All Greeks know what is right but only Spartans do it'.

Cyrus the Persian despised the Spartans because he thought them traders and shopkeepers. When they warned him to leave the Greeks alone he replied: 'I have never yet been afraid of any men who have a set place in the middle of their city where they come together to cheat each other and tell lies.' There were not many who would have agreed with him. Even the bravest opponent felt fear when the red-coated Spartiates moved into battle, performing their complicated drill. Few Spartans were ever defeated. Those that were beaten died where they stood. It was Sparta's proud boast that its soldiers never turned their back upon an enemy, so all their wounds were in the front. Its citizens left no beautiful temples or interesting plays but today fit, tough people are still sometimes called Spartans.

An early Greek soldier

24 Gods and Sportsmen

The Greeks learned much from the people they met on their travels. This is clear from their religion, because we find them worshipping gods similar to those of Egypt, Crete and other places. Like most ancient peoples, they explained natural forces by saying they were the work of a god or goddess. The sea was controlled by one; the land was ruled by another. A rich harvest meant that the earth goddess was pleased.

Besides such simple ideas, the Greeks believed that all virtues or skills were god given. Wisdom and beauty had gods too, so had wine, laughing and dancing. When they wished to explain something exceptional in a man they gave credit to the gods. Homer told of the great warrior Achilles who had been far stronger than other Greeks. This was not luck. It was because the gods favoured him.

The Greeks knew a great deal about their gods through Homer's writings, just as we learn about Christ from the Bible. Since Homer was writing about Mycenaean gods such beliefs were obviously very old. Perhaps because the Greeks felt very near to their gods they thought of them as having human ways. Frequently they made up fanciful tales about them which rather shocked later peoples. They lived, it was said, on Mount Olympus, whose snow-capped summit could be seen from many parts of Greece. Here they behaved very much like the Greeks themselves, scheming, quarrelling, loving and hating.

To Greeks, religion was a public thing. Its ceremonies were usually to do with their city or trade. Because of this, they tried to make every action of their lives a tribute to the gods. Each polis had its own god and held local festivals in his or her honour. No war could be won without their help.

To find out the gods' wishes Greeks consulted the *Pythia,* or priestess, at Delphi. This lady sacrificed animals to the gods and kept a careful eye open for anything which might be a sign from heaven. For example, a mouse gnawing through a bag or a cock crowing were bad signs. While in a trance she was thought to tell what the gods wanted. These divine words, or oracles, were interpreted by priests who spoke in a kind of poetry.

A Greek prayed standing up. His arms were raised with the palms of his hands turned upwards if he was thinking of the gods of heaven and downwards if he was speaking to the gods of the underworld. He talked to them as a man might talk to a close friend. But never for a moment did he forget the grim power they had over his life.

The Pantheon

The Greeks' ideas about their gods' powers varied from century to century. Zeus, the chief god, for instance, gradually grew less fierce

Bronze head of a Greek god. It may be Poseidon (ruler of the sea) or Zeus (father of the gods)

as time went on. Gods also varied from one town to another. A Spartan's idea of Athena, for example, was far different from what an Athenian thought about her. Nevertheless, these main gods, called the *Pantheon,* were worshipped as a sort of family.

Zeus, father of the gods and men.
Poseidon, ruler of the sea.
Apollo, god of sun, music and prophecy.
Athena, goddess of wisdom and the arts of peace.
Demeter, goddess of the earth.
Hera, Zeus's wife and goddess of marriage.
Hephaestus, god of fire and metal work.
Hermes, messenger of the gods and ruler of the winds.
Artemis, goddess of the moon and hunting.
Hestia, goddess of the home.
Ares, god of war.
Aphrodite, goddess of love and beauty.
Dionysus, god of wine and plays.

Only the chief gods, or Olympians, belonged to the Pantheon. There was also *Pan*, the god of the flocks and woodlands, and numerous semi-godlike creatures such as Naiads, who lived in the waters, and Dryads, who lived in the trees. Indeed, in the Greek world there were almost as many gods as people! The city year was full of religious festivals. Laws began with a tribute to the gods and every meeting with a prayer. Most cities had favourite gods and even important families sometimes claimed to have a minor god as their founder.

Pelops' bride

Religious ceremonies could take many forms. Solemn sacrifices, processions, theatrical performances and even sporting events were all festivals. The most famous sporting occasion was the Olympic Games. As with so many other happenings, the Greeks told a story to explain how these had begun.

Long ago a certain King Oenamaus had been blessed with a beautiful daughter, Hippodamia, whom many men wished to marry. To win her the king decreed that they must beat him in a fifty-mile chariot race from Elis (where the Games were later held) to Corinth. Many tried but all failed because the King's chariot was drawn by magic horses. Then one lover, Pelops, bribed the royal charioteer to fix pins made of wax instead of metal in the wheels. Not surprisingly, the King's chariot broke down. Pelops won the race, married Hippodamia and when she died held funeral sports in her honour.

By 776 B.C. athletic meetings were taking place at Olympia, where temples and stadiums were built from the ruins of an old city. Eventually one of the most beautiful of all Greek temples was erected there. Here sportsmen from all over the Greek world gathered every four years after heralds had journeyed from city to city, ordering any wars to stop temporarily. This 'Olympic truce' enabled all the athletes to reach the Games safely. Once there they lived in tents, lit camp fires and put up stalls for food.

An athlete removes oil put
on his body after he has
exercised. He is using
a scraper called a strigil

The Olympic Games

At first only foot races were held. The enclosure for these was one
stadion (about 606 feet) in length and 90 feet wide. From this we
get the word, stadium. The runners ran up and down in a straight
line, not round a circular track as they do today. The starter had no
whistle but a stick which he used to beat any runner who started
too soon. In later times javelin-throwing, boxing, wrestling, chariot
and mule racing were added. The sports began when, 'the Eagle rose
and the Dolphin dived'. This sounds mysterious but probably referred
to the raising of a wooden beam with a model dolphin on one end
and an eagle on the other.

Certain contests involved more than one skill. The *Pentathlon*,
for example, combined running, long jumping, wrestling, javelin
and discus throwing. Jumpers carried small weights which they
thought made them leap further. Javelins were hurled from a leather
strap held between the fingers. The discus was about eight inches
in diameter and weighed 6 pounds. Some events were very rough.
The *Pancration* was unarmed combat with eye gouging, arm twisting,
and kicking allowed. Men occasionally died as a result. Most
exciting and dangerous was the nine-mile chariot race. Sometimes
as many as forty chariots took part. The five-day festival ended with
the winners being crowned with sacred olive wreaths and all the
athletes parading in the moonlight, singing hymns.

A champion sportsman could be sure of a great reception when
he returned home. Everybody turned out to see him. Once or twice
grateful citizens pulled down part of the wall to let a favourite
athlete in. His name was recorded in a golden book and he was
allowed to wear purple robes like a king. This was because to the
Greeks such a man represented the power of the gods on earth. In
their opinion, only those whom the gods loved could win at the
Olympics.

25 The Persian Wars

Marathon •

Burial Mound

Persi
Fleet

The Greeks enjoyed many centuries of self-rule before they were conquered, first by Macedon and later by Rome. Before this the only serious threat came from Persia. The empire founded by Cyrus the Great has already been mentioned. By 490 B.C. it had reached as far as Asia Minor, where certain Greek colonies were overrun. Soon afterwards King Darius, Cyrus's grandson, demanded obedience from Athens and Sparta. These cities refused so he sent an army to punish them. When his men landed near the plain of Marathon the Athenians, accompanied by men from another city, Plataea, marched out to meet them. The Spartans did not come because they were celebrating a festival. We know a great deal about the wars which followed because a Greek historian, Herodotus, wrote an account which still exists.

It took a great deal of courage to face a Persian army at that time. Persian troops had conquered most of the Middle Eastern world. Although they were in some ways a more cultured people than the Greeks, they were noted for their fighting skill. At Marathon they far outnumbered the tiny Athenian force. Even so, a Greek army had certain advantages over other troops of the time. A Greek *hoplite* (infantryman) was heavily armed. He carried a spear, shield and sword, was protected by a helmet which covered most of his face, and wore a metal or leather breast plate. All Greek men were highly trained soldiers. The average Athenian, for example, was likely to spend nearly forty years doing military duties of one kind or another. A compact force of these soldiers, moving in formation and inspired by a favourable sign from the gods was difficult to beat.

Marathon

The men of Athens were lined up on hills overlooking a swampy plain. The Persians had their backs to the sea. By custom, a different general commanded the Greeks each day. Five refused to give battle because they thought the signs unfavourable. On the sixth day it was the turn of Miltiades. At dawn he formed his hoplites into a long line, four deep in the centre and eight deep on either wing.

Chanting a war hymn to Apollo, the Greeks came down the hill at a run. They crashed at speed into the Persian ranks and began to hack and slash at close quarters. It was an historic moment. 'Until this time no Greek could hear the word Persian without terror', comments Herodotus. The Persians tried to counter-attack but when they drove forward into the weak Greek centre they found themselves surrounded by each wing. With their cavalry useless on such marshy ground and their poorly protected bowmen massacred at close quarters, they were defeated.

A hoplite's helmet. It was beaten from a single sheet of bronze and the secret of doing this remains undiscovered to this day

Plan of the Battle of Marathon

When the Greeks saw their enemies climb into their ships and sail away, they were overjoyed. Six thousand, four hundred Persians lay dead on the field of Marathon; only 192 Athenians had fallen. During the battle Pheidippides, a hoplite who was also a famous runner, ran to Athens with the news and then on to Sparta to get help. Altogether he covered just over 140 miles before dropping dead from exhaustion. Nowadays the longest race (26 miles, roughly the distance from Marathon to Athens) is called a Marathon. Meanwhile the Spartans had finished their festival and marched at great speed to the scene. Herodotus remarked: 'They came, however, too late for the battle; yet, as they had a longing to behold the Medes (Persians), they continued their march to Marathon and there viewed the slain.'

Darius was furious when he heard the news. He decided to lead a much larger army against Greece but died before he could do so. His son, Xerxes, was as determined as his father to punish the Greeks. The army he assembled was so enormous that it amazed the civilised world. Herodotus wrote that it was drawn from forty-six nations and consisted of 5,283,000 men. He describes how Xerxes had to use a special system to count so many soldiers. Ten thousand men were made to stand close together so that a circular line could be drawn round them. Then a fence was erected on this line and the enclosure filled up with successive ten thousands until the entire army had been counted.

Certainly these numbers and such tales are exaggerated. Xerxes' army probably had not more than 150,000 soldiers. Nevertheless, it is clear that by the winter of 481 B.C. a very large army and fleet had been assembled at Sardis. Next spring it crossed the Hellespont on a long bridge made of boats tied stem to stern. For seven days and seven nights the Great King watched his men cross into Europe. A few tiny cities stood between him and the mastery of another continent.

Thermopylae

The Spartans, too busy to come to Marathon, entered the fight quickly this time. One of their kings, Leonidas, took three hundred picked men and led troops drawn from other Greek cities to the narrow pass of Thermopylae (Hot Springs), the only way through the mountains which divide northern and central Greece. Xerxes sent his Immortals repeatedly into the narrow gorge but each time they were forced back. For three days Leonidas and his men held out. Then a Greek traitor showed the Persians a narrow pathway round the Greek positions.

As the Persians poured into the valley behind the Greeks, Leonidas ordered all but the Spartiates to escape. Most went but the Thespian and Theban armies stayed with the Spartans. Of these, the Thespians and Spartans fought to the end, first with their spears and swords and, when these were broken, with hands and teeth until all were dead. Years afterwards the grateful Greeks erected a stone over their graves. On it was inscribed 'Stranger, tell the Spartans that we lie here obedient to their laws'.

26 Salamis and Victory

Thermopylae had merely delayed the Persians. Now the whole Greek world was in danger. Anxiously, the Athenians consulted the oracle at Delphi. At first the Pythian priestess was most discouraging. 'Save yourselves and bow your heads in grief', she moaned. When questioned a second time she was more hopeful, saying 'Safe shall the wooden wall continue for thee and thy children. Wait not the tramp of the horse, nor the footmen mightily moving over the land, but turn your back to the foe, and retire ye.' This led to much discussion. Some were sure it meant they should build a wooden fence round the city. Themistocles, the Athenian leader, thought it meant ships.

A few years before the Athenians had found silver at Sunium. With this new wealth they had built and equipped a fine navy. Perhaps the priestess meant that they should give up the city, retire to the islands nearby and fight a battle with the Persian fleet? It was a difficult decision to make but few Athenians doubted that it was their one chance. The alternative was surrender and any one who suggested that was executed. Only the guardians of the temples on the Acropolis remained in the city; everybody else retired

Athenian coin. The silver for it came from Sunium. The owl was a symbol of the goddess Athena

Greek warship overtaking a merchant ship

to the islands. The Athenian fleet, reinforced by other Greek navies, prepared to fight a sea battle in the narrow waters between the island of Salamis and the mainland.

Xerxes felt sure of victory. He occupied Athens and burned it, killing all the temple priests. Sadly the Athenians watched their city in flames. Across the waters they saw the masts of over a thousand Persian war galleys. There seemed little hope, but they decided to fight.

Salamis

On Salamis the Greek admirals debated what to do. Should they go out and attack the Persians in the open sea, or fight in the Straits? The commander from Corinth was cautious. 'In the Games', he warned, 'those who start too soon are whipped.' In his opinion they should avoid battle as long as possible. Themistocles was annoyed at this. 'And those who start too late win no prizes.' he replied boldly. He wanted to force a fight in the Straits where their smaller numbers would not be such a handicap. Most of the admirals agreed with him.

The problem was how to get the Persians to come in. This was solved in a cunning manner. Themistocles sent a messenger pretending to be a traitor. This man informed Xerxes that the Greek fleet intended to escape. Hurriedly, the Persian King ordered two hundred of his ships to block the exit on the other side of the island. Then his weakened main force was told to enter the Straits as soon as possible in case the Greeks got away. On the day of the battle Persian lookouts saw a single line of Greek warships rowing out from behind the cliffs. Battle lines were formed hurriedly and three columns of Persian ships moved forward. As they did so the Greeks reversed back into the Straits. Xerxes' war galleys followed— straight into a trap.

The Greeks used their rams to smash deep into the enemy ships. Then they boarded them so that their hoplites could massacre the poorly armed Persian, Phoenician and Egyptian sailors. Vessels rolled over or broke in two. Javelins, arrows and even stones knocked

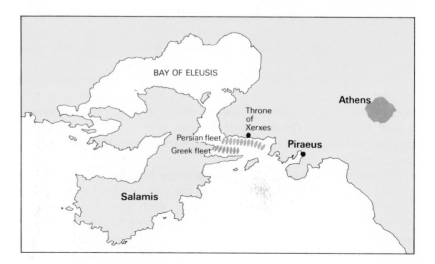

Plan of the Battle of Salamis

men down on the crowded, often sinking ships. All day the struggle continued until the sea was littered with wreckage. An Athenian poet, Aeschylus, fought in the battle. Afterwards he wrote of how:

> The sea vanished
> Under a clogged carpet of shipwrecks,
>   limbs, torsos [bodies].
> No sea, and the beaches were cluttered
>   with dead.

Seated on a special throne, Xerxes watched with horror. He saw his ships so crushed together that one often sank another. Frequently he jumped up and cried out. In the evening, after his fleet had retired, the Greeks massacred all the enemy sailors they could find. The proud Persian fleet had suffered such a severe defeat that it could no longer guard the army's long supply lines. Xerxes was forced to retreat from Europe. For forty-five days his troops marched wearily back into Asia. Only a picked force of Immortals led by Mardonius remained in northern Greece.

Plataea

Salamis had saved the Greek world from a foreign dictator, but the Greeks were soon quarrelling among themselves again. It was only after much grumbling that they gathered an army to face Mardonius at all. Indeed, they might never have fought had not the Persian cavalry captured their food supplies as they sat in camp at Plataea. Faced with starvation, they reluctantly formed battle lines and came out to meet the Persians.

At first things went badly for the Greeks. Wave after wave of fierce Immortals shattered their lines. In this crisis only the Spartan troops stood firm. Through the din of clashing swords, groans and shouts, the deep Spartiate voices could be heard chanting a war hymn. 'Come now young men, do battle, each keeping his place in the line. . . . Forget love of life when you confront the foe. Let each withstand the onset . . . his two feet firmly planted on the ground, biting his lip with his teeth.' In spite of such courage, the Spartan army might well have been destroyed but for a stroke of luck. Mardonius could be seen clearly on a white horse. Suddenly a Spartan broke through his guard and smashed his head at a blow. As the news of their commander's death spread, the Persian ranks broke and fled.

That night the Spartan leader sat in Xerxes' own war tent and ordered the Persian cooks to prepare the sort of meal their king had liked. Then he put a simple Spartan meal beside it and remarked, 'I sent for you, O Greeks, to show you the folly of this Median captain [Xerxes] who, when he enjoyed such food as this, must needs come here to rob us'.

All over the Greek world the gods were honoured. At Delphi a lovely column was erected. At Plataea the victory was celebrated for centuries at a special festival. Solemnly each year the Plataeans would drink a toast 'to those who lost their lives for the freedom of Hellas'.

27 Pericles and The Golden Age

Bust of Pericles

An *Ostrakon*. You can see the name Themistocles

What was the freedom for which these men died? Not all Greeks took as active a part in their government as the Athenians. Nevertheless, all were ruled by laws which even their leaders obeyed. This was the difference between the Greeks and other peoples. The Persian king's own actions were not tied by his country's laws. He might take advice from his satraps but no one dared disobey him. Millions of men and women jumped like puppets when one man pulled the strings. The Greeks thought this was stupid.

Government by the people (democracy) began in Athens around 507 B.C., when the town was divided into three sections for voting purposes. Each section was split into thirty parishes and each parish was ruled by a council called the *Demes,* meaning the people. In this way power was shared amongst as many men as possible instead of being concentrated into the hands of a few. All important government jobs were filled by drawing lots.

To prevent anyone from becoming too powerful, members of the Assembly were allowed to write down on a piece of broken pot called an *Ostrakon* the name of any man they thought should leave the city. If six thousand citizens wrote the same name, this man had to leave the city for ten years. Such an exile was called Ostracism, from Ostrakon.

Pericles

To lead the independent and quarrelsome Greeks was not easy and only men of great ability ever held power for long. Such a man was Pericles who dominated Athens about ten years after the Persian Wars. Handsome, well educated and a fine speaker, he was lucky to rule the town at such a time.

The Athenians were overjoyed at their victory. However, to a foreigner there must have seemed little to rejoice about. The Acropolis hill was covered with blackened temple ruins. Athena herself was being worshipped in a temporary wooden shrine. The houses huddled at the foot of the hill were dirty slums set in smelly alleys. Wild dogs roamed about, rubbish was left to rot in the streets, pigs lived in the gardens and the marshes to the south were infested with mosquitos which caused malaria. Yet Athens, led by Pericles, was about to enjoy its Golden Age.

Athens had led the Greeks in war. Now it forced many of them to follow in peacetime. A league of Greek states was formed with its treasury at Delos and its headquarters at Athens. Later the silver at Delos was moved to Athens. Eventually this Athenian league of city states stretched from Greece to Sicily, Italy, Egypt and Cyprus. Only Sparta kept apart and formed its own league. Piraeus, the port of Athens, is some way from the city itself, so a defensive wall was

built between the two. This wall followed the route of an earlier one built by Themistocles. It was made of stone and stretched for four miles. Supreme at sea, the Athenians were determined not to be cut off from their fleet by a land enemy.

Like most Greeks, Pericles was ready for war if necessary. For example, he sent an expedition to Egypt to help a revolt against Persian rule. But he hoped for peace so that he could make Athens the most beautiful city in the world. The Persian wars had shown that Athens was great. Pericles wished to build signs of this greatness for all to see. 'What I desire is that you should fix your eyes every day on the greatness of Athens as she really is, and that you should fall in love with her,' he said. Every stone laid or carved, every statue painted was to be in honour of the gods who had given Athens victory. In his Greek way Pericles was inviting the citizens to join him in an act of worship.

The Parthenon

Pericles was in charge of the work, with architects, Ictinus and Callicrates, and a sculptor, Phidias, as his assistants. Almost every craftsman or workman helped in some way or another. On the Acropolis, the Parthenon, a wonderful temple to Athena was erected. Originally it was 228 feet long, 101 feet wide and 65 feet high with 58 main columns and over 500 carved figures. All its lines appear to be straight but in fact all are curved. This is because Ictinus knew that

really straight lines would appear to sag. Thus, every column bulges out slightly and all slope inwards. Today its ruined yellow stones shine bare and bright in the sun. When built it was a blaze of colour. On the pediments its stone figures were painted with gold hair, pink faces, and scarlet and emerald garments, all against a glowing blue background.

The Parthenon was only one of the beauties of the Acropolis. Around it stood other buildings, including a small blue and white temple called the Erechtheum which housed sacred relics. A huge gold and ivory statue of Athena stood on a high point so that sailors miles out at sea could see the sun flashing on her gold helmet and know that they were nearly home. The Propylaea, an impressive gateway, dominated the entrance to the hill. Down in the town graceful walks were built around the Agora. Overlooking this market place was the Theseum, a temple similar to the Parthenon, built in honour of the god Hephaestus. This is the only ancient Greek building to survive well preserved to the present-day.

Before Pericles died the greatest days of Athens were ending. Plague had struck its citizens. It was beginning a long and disastrous war with Sparta. But Pericles' wish did come true. For centuries visitors have gazed at what his people did and most have fallen in love with Athens.

Left: Ruins of the Parthenon

Below left: A column from the Erechtheum

Plan of Athens

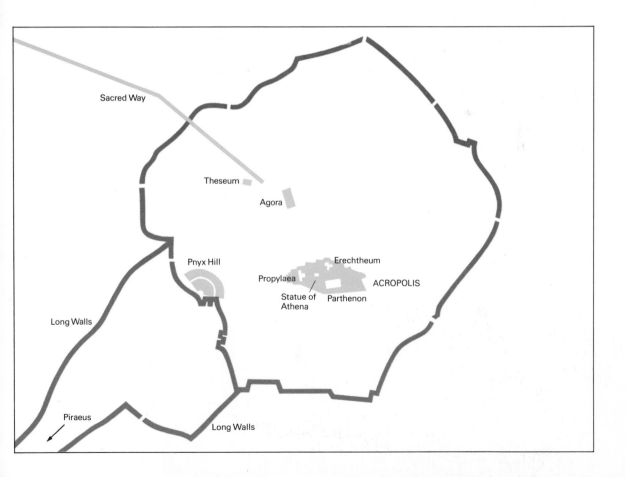

Greece is a sunny land so there is little need to make homes warm and comfortable. The poorer Athenians mostly lived in small box-like dwellings with few windows and a single door opening on to the street. Town houses were usually one or two storeys high. They were built of brick on a stone base and had tiled sloping roofs. The larger ones had courtyards. The upper storey was for the women's use because they were rarely allowed out. On the other hand, men were away a lot so a guard or porter was employed to protect the house. He sat in a porch or cupboard just inside the main entrance.

Food was always simple, but among the rich meals lasted a long time. Few races have loved conversation as much as the Greeks. To prevent all the diners talking at once a president was usually elected for the evening. His job was to organise the discussion and keep order. Although this after-dinner discussion was called the *Symposium* (drinking together) the Greeks drank little except at festival times. Wine was nearly always mixed with water because, as one Greek wrote, 'The first cup means health, the second pleasure, the third is for sleep and then wise men go home. The fourth means rudeness, the fifth shouting, and the sixth disorder in the streets, the seventh black eyes and the eighth a police summons.'

Ancient Greece was very much a man's world. Shut away at home, women took no part in politics. They did not belong to the Assembly and could not vote. Girls of well-to-do families were educated at home by their mothers. This rarely amounted to much. One Greek writer, describing the childhood of a certain girl, said she was brought up, 'under the strictest restraint, in order that she might see as little, hear as little, and ask as few questions as possible'. Soon after her fifteenth birthday a girl was usually married to a man chosen by her parents. Only at wedding and festival feasts did men and women dine together. After a marriage ceremony cakes made from sesame seeds and honey were eaten.

Dining scene painted on a pot

Boys started their education at about seven years of age. They were led to school by a slave called a *paedagogos* (boy-keeper). If they did not walk fast enough, or tried to run away, he beat them. Nevertheless, a Greek boy's schooldays seem to have been quite pleasant. The main subject was Homer's two long poems, the *Iliad* and *Odyssey*. As well as teaching a boy Greek history, these books told him about the gods. Homer's lines were learnt by heart and frequently recited aloud. Other lessons, such as wrestling, physical training and even the Greek language, often took place to the sound of music. The chief musical instrument was the stringed lyre, but country folk played simple pipes. Spelling lessons were sometimes turned into plays with boys representing different letters.

Writing was scratched on a wax pad with a *stylus*, a pointed stick tipped with iron or bone. Its top was flattened for smoothing out mistakes on the wax surface. Counting was done with the fingers or on an abacus (reckoning board). This was a wooden frame with three lines of beads stretched across it. On the top line each bead represented one, on the second, ten, and on the third, a hundred. In their free time Greek children played games surprisingly like those of today. They spun tops and rolled hoops, enjoyed many kinds of ball games and tossed five small bones into the air, catching them on the backs of their hands.

By this time the old cuneiform and picture writing was growing out of date. The Phoenicians had created an alphabet of twenty-four letters. Its first letter was *aleph* and its second *beth*; this is how we get the word 'alphabet'. The Greeks copied the Phoenicians but added vowels. The Roman and most modern alphabets are based on that of the Greeks which was as follows:

as it was written in Pericles' time	as it is written today	names of the Greek letters	the nearest English letters
A	A	alpha	A
B	B	beta	B
∧	Γ	gamma	G
Δ	Δ	delta	D
E	E	epsilon	E (short)
I	Z	zeta	Z SD
H	H	eta	E (long) H
⊙	Θ	theta	Th
I	I	iota	I
K	K	kappa	K
∨	Λ	lambda	L
M	M	mu	M
N	N	nu	N
XϚ or XE	Ξ	xi	X KS
O	O	omicron	O (short)
Γ	Π	pi	P
P or R	P	rho	R
ϟ or Ϟ	Σ	sigma	S
T	T	tau	T
V	Y	upsilon	U
Φ	Φ	phi	Ph, F
X	X	khi	Kh, Ch
ΦϚ or ΦE	Ψ	psi	Ps
Ω	Ω	omega	O (long)

The Greek calendar was a lunar one with the year divided into a series of religious festivals. Usually there were twelve months of thirty days, but if a month had twenty-nine days the news was announced by a town crier. This frequently confused both children and adults, especially as individual towns sometimes had different calendars.

Soldiers and craftsmen

After school a boy went for military training. The Greeks regarded life as a continuous struggle. They loved liberty, were extremely quarrelsome and believed that no city was entitled to be free if it was not ready to fight. Therefore war played an important part in their lives. At first young men were full-time soldiers for two years during which they served both at home and abroad. Then they retired to civilian life but could be called up for active service at any time up to the age of sixty. Military leaders were elected like leaders in civilian life.

With such a warlike attitude it is surprising that Athens did not become a city of soldiers. In fact, the Athenians devoted as much time as possible to peaceful occupations. The city itself was made beautiful, as we have seen, by the efforts of its citizens. Above all, it was a town of small craftsmen. Sword makers, sculptors, stone-masons, potters and blacksmiths all lived and worked in its noisy streets and market places.

Pottery was a particularly important trade. The clay of Attica turns an orange red colour when baked. This is called *terracotta*. In early times black patterns and figures were painted on this red background. Pottery of the Golden Age is usually the opposite—glossy black with red figures. The Greeks loved pots of different shapes and sizes, each for a particular purpose. There was, for example, a pot for wine, another for water and yet another for mixing the two before meals. Other *amphorae,* as they were called, were used for the storage of food and oil. Many are beautifully shaped and their decorations tell us a great deal about Greek dress, religion and ways of life.

Above all, the Greeks loved talking. All political action took place as a result of a debate and the art of speaking (oratory) was taught at school. If a Greek was not drunk with wine, he was certainly drunk with words.

This Greek pot which was used for holding water or wine shows a scene from Homer's story *The Iliad.* Hector, the Trojan hero, has been killed by Achilles and his body is being dragged behind his chariot

29 Plays, Books and Writers

The Greeks had many festivals. Like most farmers, they celebrated the spring and harvest. Later, festivals were held to honour the gods. Some, like the Olympic Games, were devoted to sport. Others stressed music, dancing, acting and mime. From these developed theatrical performances. At first there were no individual actors. Instead, a number of people, the *Chorus*, chanted or recited a story. Later an actor, usually the poet, helped them to tell the tale. After the Persian Wars the Athenian dramatist Aeschylus wrote plays with two separate characters as well as the Chorus. In this way conversation, or dialogue, became possible.

The first religious festivals were probably performed in the village hall. Then special theatres were built. Since Greece has a dry climate these were open air. Around a circular space called the *Orchestra*, seats were set in a series of semi-circles, each raised above the one in front so that all the spectators could see clearly. Early theatres were built of wood but after several disastrous fires the Athenians decided

The theatre at Epidaurus. It is still used for plays today

to make them of stone. For this reason some have survived to the present-day.

Most of these were much larger than modern theatres. The one at Epidaurus seated 17,000 and was more like a sports stadium. In spite of their size, they were so well constructed that even the smallest sound could be heard in the back row. The actors wore large masks because their faces could not be seen at a distance. This also meant that they could perform several different parts in the same play.

Playwrights and philosophers

The Greeks sometimes wrote funny plays. *The Wasps* by Aristophanes pokes fun at the people of his day. It was also the custom for a short humorous play to follow three serious ones. Nevertheless, most Greek plays are tragedies which tell grim stories about the gods. Aeschylus, for example, told of the Persian Wars but made it a sad tale by concentrating on Xerxes. Thus instead of celebrating a Greek victory, he wrote of how the proud Persian failed because he dared to imitate the gods. Sophocles, another dramatist, chose to tell how a certain King Oedipus was doomed one day accidentally to kill his father and marry his mother. When he discovers what he has done he blinds himself.

As well as honouring the gods, the Greeks loved to ask questions about life. Socrates, their greatest philosopher (lover of wisdom) was an ugly, clumsy man who would stop passers-by and ask questions such as, 'What is love?' or 'What is justice?' Some people were merely

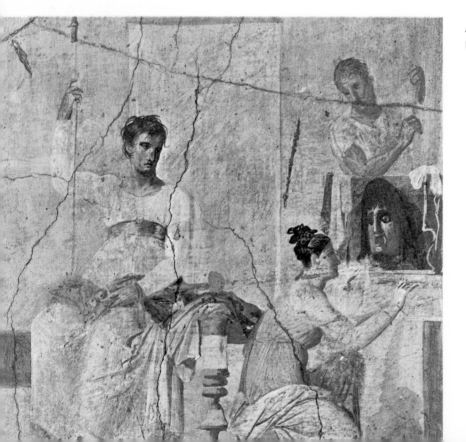

A tragic actor: notice his mask on the right

Socrates

annoyed and hurried on. Others found themselves forced to think deeply about such matters for the first time. Socrates wrote nothing, but a lot of what he said was written down by several of his pupils, particularly Plato. Plato's writings are not always an accurate account of Socrates' opinions but thanks to him we can read some of the fascinating conversations the philosopher had with his friends more than 2,000 years ago.

Such an outspoken man made enemies. After the Spartans had defeated Athens (see Chapter 30) the new government set up in the city accused him of leading young people astray with his talk. He was sentenced to death and, though he could easily have escaped from prison, he refused to do so because it would have meant breaking the laws of his city. He died bravely, talking to his friends even as he sipped the cup of poison.

Plato was different from his famous master. Handsome and rich, he wrote poems and plays, and studied science. He was also less friendly and pleasure-loving than Socrates. His keen interest in politics led him to start a school for statesmen. Yet, his only attempt to train a real statesman, Dionysus of Syracuse, was a failure. His book, *The Republic,* describes what he thought to be a perfect state. This book is written as a number of discussions between Socrates and his friends.

Socrates' curiosity caused him to argue. Another inquiring Greek, Aristotle, preferred to gather as much information as possible about the world around him. 'All men possess by nature the desire to know,' he wrote. It was certainly true of himself. Altogether he is said to have written 146 books. The few which survive show that nothing was too serious or trivial for Aristotle. For example, there is one 'On Alexander' (see Chapter 31), another 'On drunkeness' and a third 'On being given in marriage'. Yet he also wrote important books about literature, politics and the art of public speaking. No Greek had more influence on the people of the Middle Ages than Aristotle. He was thought to be always right and was called 'the Philosopher'. Actually in small matters he could be wrong. He thought, for instance, that goats breathed through their ears.

The Greeks' curiosity led to many discoveries. Pythagoras and his pupils laid down various rules in geometry. Pythagoras himself also declared the world to be round when many thought it was flat. Euclid wrote out the geometrical rules which are still learnt as theorems in school. Aristarches was the first man to suggest that the earth and planets moved around the sun, instead of the other way round.

Another Greek scientist, Archimedes of Syracuse, realised as he sat in his bath that a body placed in water displaces the same volume of water as itself. Delighted he jumped out naked and ran through the streets shouting 'Eureka, Eureka' (I've found it). Hippocrates was the first famous Greek doctor. He founded a hospital and wrote books on medicine. His habit of keeping a careful watch on a patient and recording every symptom is the basis of medical practice to this day.

The Greeks not only asked questions. Frequently they answered them as well. In this way they widened the boundaries of knowledge.

30 The Fall of Athens

Even before Pericles died a long war between Sparta and Athens divided the Greek world. Few cities managed to stay out of this Peloponnesian War which lasted twenty-seven years. As well as being a struggle between a sea power (Athens) and a land power (Sparta), it was a struggle between the Athenian love of personal freedom and the Spartan belief that a citizen's first duty was to serve his state. In addition Spartan merchants were jealous of the Athenians' control of so much trade in the eastern Mediterranean. The story of their long fight was written by Thucydides, who himself took part in it.

Pericles felt sure that if the Athenians avoided fighting the Spartans and attacked Sparta's allies instead, they would win. Athens with its long walls was difficult to capture. It was richer than Sparta and so would be able to fight longer. Unfortunately, Athens had a weakness; it depended on supplies of corn from south Russia. Should this 'life-line' be cut its people would starve. Every time the Athenian Assembly met during the war it discussed this vital problem.

The leaders after Pericles did not follow his wise advice. They wasted money on expensive naval expeditions as well as fighting the Spartans on land. Plague broke out in Athens while it was being besieged and an army sent to attack Syracuse was wiped out. These setbacks broke Athenian power, and led to disaster. In 405 B.C. the Spartan admiral Lysander smashed the Athenian fleet in a battle in the Hellespont and so cut the corn route.

Only nine war-galleys escaped Lysander's men and of these one, the *Paralus*, sailed back to Athens. An eye-witness described the sad scene when it returned. 'It was night when the *Paralus* reached Athens with her evil tidings, and a bitter wail of woe broke forth. From Piraeus, following the line of the long wall up to the heart of the city, it [the wailing] swept and swelled, as each man passed the news to his neighbour. On that night no man slept.'

Corinth, Sparta's ally, wished to destroy Athens completely, killing all the men and selling the women and children as slaves. The Spartans, however, remembered how the Athenians had saved the Greek world at Marathon and Salamis and refused to allow such a massacre. Nevertheless, they occupied the city, destroyed the long wall and reduced the once mighty Athenian navy to twelve ships. For a time the inhabitants were ruled through a government called the Thirty. Fortunately, before many years had passed, democratic rule returned to Athens. Although never a great power again, it regained much trade and the people rebuilt the city walls. Athens did not cease to be famous for art, philosophy and literature. Socrates was still alive when the war ended. So were Sophocles

The harbour at Syracuse
as it is today

and other famous Greek dramatists. Sparta, meanwhile, tried to form a league of Greek cities but failed. Thebes became the leading city for a few years.

Philip of Macedon

While the Greeks wasted time and energy quarrelling amongst themselves, a new power arose in the north. Macedon was mountainous land inhabited by tough shepherds. Its king, Philip, knew that the successful Theban army had used spears eighteen feet long, fighting in a *phalanx* (formation) eight rows deep. He copied these tactics but increased the rows to sixteen and the spears to twenty-one feet. These Macedonian phalanxes cut through the enemy like a modern tank, leaving gaps which could be entered by the cavalry. Philip's fierce horsemen were called the Companions. They were recruited from Macedon's noblemen, and mounted on half wild ponies. Few soldiers could withstand their attacks and the Macedonian army soon proved unbeatable.

Philip must have been a frightening sight. He limped from an old wound, had only one eye and a hunched back caused by a broken collar bone. Yet he was more than just a rough warrior. The Macedonian King admired the civilised ways of cities like Athens. He was also a cunning politician who was determined to gain control of Greece. Year after year he schemed and plotted, turning the quarrelsome Greek cities against each other. Finally, when the Athenians formed a league against him he crushed their freedom once and for all at the Battle of Chaeronea (338 B.C.)

The lion of Chaeronea; a statue put up on the site of the battle

Alexander, Philip's son, had just been sent to Athens when the old warrior king himself was murdered. The whole Greek world sighed with relief at his death. In fact, as one wise man remarked, Philip's death had only reduced the Macedonian army by one! Within months the new king, Alexander, had crushed a revolt in Thessaly, after cutting steps up a mountain side to get his troops behind the enemy. Rebellious Thebes was captured and utterly destroyed. Then he conquered some fierce Balkan tribes by ferrying his army across the river Danube on leather tent covers stuffed with hay. People quickly realised that the son was more dangerous than the father.

Alexander was a strange mixture. From his mother Olympias, he inherited good looks and superstitious beliefs: she worshipped woodland gods and was probably a priestess. From his father he got bravery and an athletic body which made him enjoy personal combat on the battlefield. From his teacher, the great Aristotle, he learned a love of everything Greek, including the books of Homer. A priestess said to him when young, 'My son, thou art invincible' (unbeatable). A large part of the world was about to learn this was true.

31 Alexander the Great

Philip had wanted to conquer Greece. Alexander dreamed of mastering Persia. In 334 B.C. he left Pella with a force of 35,000 men. It was an unusual army. As well as men armed with spears and swords it had clerks who kept daily accounts of everything that happened. In addition to siege towers and battering rams, it had historians, poets and geographers. Persia was being invaded by Greek art, literature and science as well as soldiers.

Against Alexander's army was 'the Kingdom of the Whole World', stretching from Egypt to the Caspian and Black Seas. It was connected by good roads and able to assemble about a million men for battle. Its bowmen and cavalry were famous; its fleet was first class. Looking magnificent in full armour topped by a white plumed helmet, the young Alexander sacrificed a bull to the god Poseidon as he crossed the Dardanelles into Asia. His troops must have wondered whether even the gods could bring victory in such a dangerous adventure.

The Great King of Persia, Darius III, certainly did not think so. At first he did not take the invasion too seriously. Only after several armies

Alexander's Empire

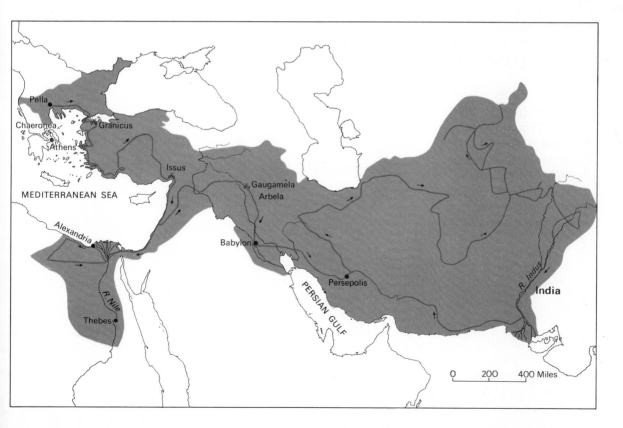

commanded by his satraps had been brushed aside did he regard it as important. Then he faced the Macedonians in person at the river Granicus. Unfortunately for him, he had placed his cavalry on a steep bank where they could not charge effectively.

When the battle started, a thrust from the Macedonian right wing led Darius to expect the real attack to come on the left. To his surprise, Alexander's right wing kept going. Charging with his spear pointed straight at his opponents' faces, Alexander himself cut down man after man, including Mithridates, Darius's son-in-law. Only once was he in danger. This was when his helmet was cut open by a Persian, but his friend, Cleitus, killed the man and so saved the king's life. Soon afterwards the Persians retreated from the battlefield and Alexander was able to occupy most of Asia Minor.

Granicus was a defeat but not a disaster for the Persians. Darius's answer was to recruit a far larger army and challenge Alexander again at Issus in 333 B.C. This time even the attacks of the Macedonian cavalry were slowed by sheer weight of numbers, until a rumour spread that Darius had fled. Although untrue, it caused the huge Persian force to crumble apart. The Macedonians were able to slaughter thousands of their enemies. Many others were captured, including Darius's wife, mother and two daughters.

That night Alexander occupied Darius's splendid war tent, a domed structure of gold cloth, delicate embroidery and precious stones. 'This, I believe, is being a King,' he remarked, as he was served with Darius's food and wine. He now claimed to be the new Great King of the Persian Empire and sent a letter containing these words to Darius, 'whenever you send to me, send to me as King of Asia . . . and if you dispute my right to the Kingdom, stay and fight another battle for it; but do not run away.'

Wall painting of the Battle of Issus. This is a Roman copy of a Greek painting. Alexander himself appears on the left bareheaded but in magnificent armour. Darius is on the right rising above the rest of his soldiers

The end of the Persian Empire

After Issus, Alexander entered Egypt where he was greeted joyfully as the enemy of the unpopular Persians. He was received with particular honour by the priests because he wore the ram horns of the god Amun in his hair. This was a cunning thing to do; it won him the favour of the Egyptians who for centuries afterwards called him the 'Two-Horned'. In fact, he was genuinely interested in Egyptian religion and may really have believed he was the son of an Egyptian god. He also showed a liking for Egyptian ways and customs and founded the city of Alexandria while he was there.

Meanwhile Darius assembled his greatest army, equipped with chariots and elephants. When the Macedonians lined up at Gaugamela, near Arbela (331 B.C.) the noise of their enemies sounded 'like the distant roaring of a mighty ocean'. Yet Alexander again proved too clever for the Persian king. First, he chose to fight on rough ground where the Persian chariots would tip over at speed. Then, when they did charge, he let them through his ranks so that his bowmen could kill the drivers. As the battle reached a dreadful climax, Alexander fought his way towards the Persian king. For a brief moment the two deadly enemies looked at each other. Then, before Alexander could strike, Darius hurled his spear and fled.

The slaughter which followed was worse than at Issus. Afterwards the victorious Macedonians raced to the great treasure city of Persepolis. This was robbed and burned in revenge for Xerxes' destruction of Athens. The Battle of Arbela destroyed the power of the Persians forever. Next year a few horsemen led by Alexander found Darius in the desert. He had been abandoned by his bodyguard and lay dying of a spear wound. A Macedonian soldier gave him a cup of water but he was dead before Alexander galloped up.

Coin showing Alexander
wearing the horns of the
Egyptian god Amun

Invasion of India

Alexander had conquered the East with his sword. In another way,
however, it was conquering him. Like his soldiers at Persepolis, its
wealth and luxury were slowly changing his character. Each day he
acted more like an eastern dictator than a Greek ruler. For example,
he expected men to touch the ground with their foreheads when they
approached him. Each day he became more cruel to those who
opposed him. Towns were ruthlessly destroyed and their inhabitants
were massacred. Even his old friend Cleitus was murdered by him
in a drunken fight and two of his generals were executed. The army,
too, was changing. After Arbela, it resembled a travelling town, with
shopkeepers, priests and actors as well as soldiers. Furthermore,
Alexander wished to go on fighting, even though Persia had been
occupied.

So the weary march east went on. In 327 B.C. the Greeks entered
India over the Himalayas. High among the tallest mountains in the
world, his men suffered from cold and hunger. When they came
down into the plains they were tormented by thirst and heat. On
one occasion they discovered a smelly and undrinkable liquid which
gushed out of the ground and burst into flames. Alexander offered
sacrifices to the gods to save his men from what was in fact oil!
Then he defeated the army of an Indian King called Porus. When this
ruler was captured and taken to Alexander the Macedonian asked
him how he expected to be treated. 'Like a King,' Porus replied
proudly. The two became allies and friends.

At last the Macedonian troops grew tired of their wanderings.
When they reached a spot near where Delhi stands today they
refused to go on. Alexander was furious but there was little he could
do. He erected a pillar for each of the Greek gods, and then began a
slow retreat. After awful experiences in the desert his men reached
Babylon. In this half-ruined city Alexander died of marsh fever just
before his thirty-third birthday (323 B.C.). When asked who should
rule after him, he whispered, 'The best'.

Naturally his generals had different ideas of who was best. In
the years of fighting which followed the empire was divided into
three main parts ruled by different generals; Antipater took Greece,
Seleucus took Babylonia and Ptolemy took Egypt.

Although his empire lasted only a short time, Alexander had opened
out the world in a way which had never happened before. Like a bee
moving from flower to flower, he had spread Greek ideas and the
Greek language far beyond Greece. After his death the Greek
influence continued and spread over all the Mediterranean lands.
Altogether he may have founded as many as seventy Greek-type
cities in the East. On the north-west frontier of India men made
and admired statues in the Greek style. In Greece itself people learned
of the ways of the Indians. Even today some people in India make
wooden carvings of Macedonian horsemen, while others talk of
Alexander as though they had known him. Year by year the legend
of Alexander has grown. In many stories he appears as a sort of god.
One can imagine how pleased he would be if he knew.

Part 8
The Roman Empire

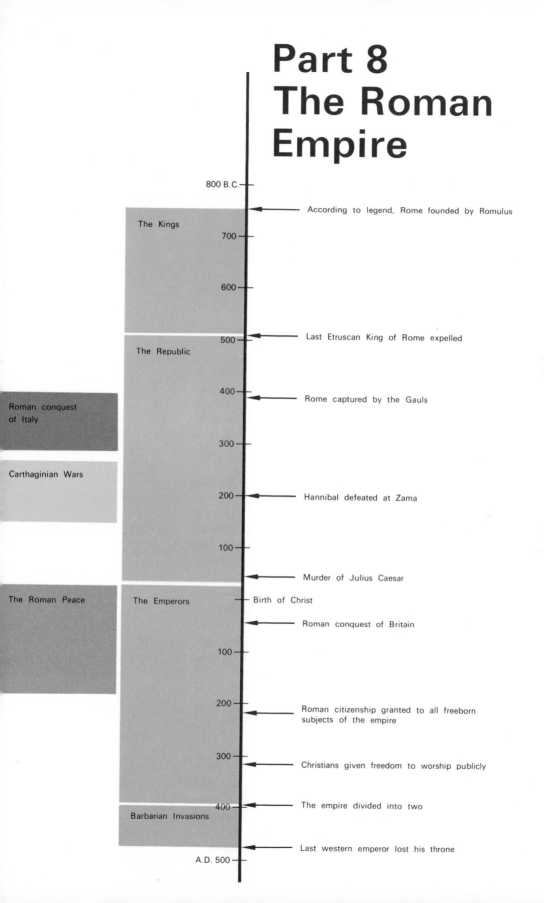

800 B.C.

According to legend, Rome founded by Romulus

The Kings

700

600

500 — Last Etruscan King of Rome expelled

The Republic

400 — Rome captured by the Gauls

Roman conquest
of Italy

300

Carthaginian Wars

200 — Hannibal defeated at Zama

100

Murder of Julius Caesar

The Roman Peace — The Emperors — Birth of Christ

Roman conquest of Britain

100

200 — Roman citizenship granted to all freeborn
subjects of the empire

300 — Christians given freedom to worship publicly

400 — The empire divided into two

Barbarian Invasions

Last western emperor lost his throne

A.D. 500

32　The City on Seven Hills

The short-lived empire of Alexander the Great was the biggest the world had known up to that time. But before long a greater and much more long-lasting empire began to grow up around the shores of the Mediterranean. Its centre was the city of Rome, situated half way down the west coast of Italy, about fifteen miles from the sea.

In the fourth century B.C., at the time of Alexander's conquests, Rome was little more than the centre of a prosperous farming area. Among its neighbours in Italy were people who were probably more powerful and certainly more civilised. But, as we shall see, Rome gradually extended its rule throughout Italy and all the lands bordering the Mediterranean.

The beginnings of Rome

Little is known about the earliest history of Rome. We are forced to rely on legends, a few findings of archaeologists and a lot of guesswork. It almost certainly began as a collection of mud huts built by peasant farmers on the south bank of the river Tiber. These farmers were called *Latins*, which means 'men of the wide plain'. Like the Greeks, they originally came from central Asia, about 2000–1500 B.C.

The position of Rome was a good one. It was surrounded by low hills, making it easy to defend, and the river was shallow enough at that point to be easily crossed. Its climate was similar to that of Greece—hot in summer, mild in winter. There was enough rain to make the soil fertile. In the plains surrounding the city plentiful crops of corn, olives, grapes and other fruits were produced. There was also good pasture for sheep and cattle.

After a while the Romans began to trade; first with neighbouring tribes, then with merchants who came by sea from North Africa, Greece and the eastern Mediterranean. Eventually a port called Ostia grew up at the mouth of the Tiber. Merchants and shopkeepers appeared in the midst of the farming community. They bought and sold food, wool and leather from the farms and some goods from overseas. Roman craftsmen learned how to make tools and weapons, pots and pans, furniture and clothing (although most families continued to spin and weave their own woollen cloth).

Rome's Italian neighbours

The Latins were just one of several tribes that entered Italy from the north, through the Alpine passes. In the upland regions to the east and north of Rome were the Samnites, Umbrians and others. These were later joined by much more civilised peoples—Etruscans and Greeks—who came by sea.

The Etruscans first settled (about 1000 B.C.) near the Latins in

Early Rome

the coastal plain north of the Tiber. They later expanded inland, pushing the Umbrians further east. We know little about the Etruscan way of life because we cannot read their inscriptions, but almost everything we have found suggests they came from Mesopotamia. Etruscans were skilful metal workers, builders and artists. They made metal boxes, beautiful statues of bronze and built painted temples

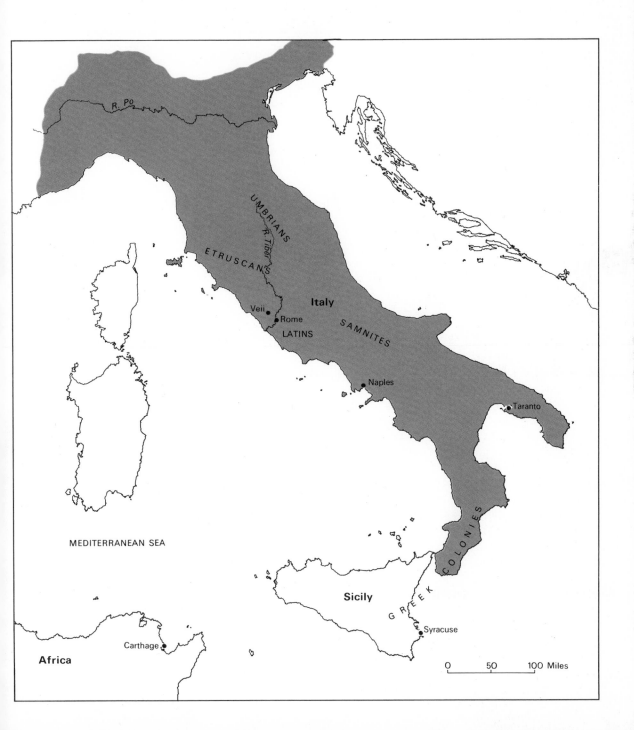

The she-wolf suckling
Romulus and Remus

out of blocks of baked earth. Above all, they excelled in the making of pottery. Josiah Wedgwood, the greatest English potter who lived 200 years ago, based some of his finest designs on Etruscan ware. He called his factory Etruria, after the land of the Etruscans.

In the eighth century B.C. Greek adventurers began to settle in southern Italy and the coastal plains of eastern Sicily. At places like Naples, Taranto and Syracuse prosperous Greek 'colonies' sprang up. Their advanced way of life and their works of art had some civilising influence on the more primitive Italian tribes in the area.

The legends of Romulus and the early kings

Centuries later, Romans made up stories about the beginnings of their city so that the people would be proud of its history. It was said that Rome had been founded in 753 B.C. by Romulus, a son of Mars, god of war. When he was a baby, Romulus, together with his twin brother Remus, was abandoned in a cradle on the Tiber—at the orders of his wicked uncle. But the twins were saved when their cradle was washed ashore. They were looked after by a she-wolf until a shepherd found them and brought them up as his own sons.

We are told that when the twins grew up they founded a city at the spot where they had been rescued. Following a quarrel, in which Remus was killed, Romulus called the new town Rome, after his own name. He made himself the first king and encouraged neighbouring farmers to come and live there. According to tradition, in the next 250 years Rome was ruled by seven kings in all. They gave the city its laws and its religion, built a bridge over the river and extended their territory. Rome had started on the slopes of what was later called the Palatine Hill, but gradually the six surrounding hills were included within its walls. This explains why it is often called 'the City on Seven Hills'.

It is said that the last king of Rome was an Etruscan called Tarquin the Proud. His rule was harsh and unpopular, and he was driven out in a rebellion (509 B.C.). Tarquin tried to recover the throne, with the help of an Etruscan prince, Lars Porsena. In his famous poem, *Horatius*, the English poet Lord Macaulay pictured the scene when the enemy approached the narrow wooden bridge over the Tiber. Horatius and two companions stood shoulder to shoulder blocking the way. They bravely held off the Etruscans until the supports of the bridge were cut down by their fellow Romans behind them. The two friends of Horatius returned to safety before the bridge collapsed. Horatius, left alone on the opposite bank, dived fully armed into the river and swam back, amid loud cheers.

Although the details of these stories were almost entirely made up, there is a small basis of truth in them. For instance, there is little doubt that Rome was once ruled by kings and that it was conquered, about this time, by the Etruscans. The largest Etruscan town, Veii, was only a dozen miles from Rome. Its people must have been attracted to the fertile plains across the Tiber. Almost certainly the last two or three kings of Rome, ending with Tarquin the Proud, were Etruscan conquerors.

Wall painting from an
Etruscan tomb. The man
is dancing and playing
a pipe

33 S.P.Q.R.

After they had driven out the Etruscans, the Roman people decided they would have no more kings. Instead, they set up a *republic*— a form of government in which rulers are usually chosen by the citizens. At that time Rome was quite small, so it was possible for most of the population to meet together in one place, as in the Greek cities. At certain times of the year—for example after the harvest had been collected—they gathered in an Assembly to elect their rulers.

The government of the republic

From now on, the Romans were determined to prevent any one man from having too much power. They therefore divided the former kings' duties between two equal magistrates called *consuls*. These were expected to keep a check on each other. If they disagreed it was possible for either one of them to cancel the other's decisions. This was called a *veto*, which is Latin for 'I forbid'. To make doubly sure that the consuls did not get too powerful they were only elected for one year.

Of course, two consuls alone could not carry out all the business

A general view of the Roman forum (market place) as it looks today

of government. Therefore the citizens' Assembly elected other ruling magistrates, including chief justices and chief constables. When their period of office was over magistrates usually became life members of the *Senate*—a council of experienced politicians which got its name from the Latin *senex*, meaning 'an old man'. This had a long history, going back to the days before the republic. The kings had been expected to listen to the advice of the Senate, although they were not forced to act upon it. Now the consuls were in the same position. But in practice the Senate had much more power in the republic. Consuls held office for such a short time that they would have been foolish to ignore the advice of men whose experience of government was greater than theirs.

As the city grew in size and became more difficult to govern, the Senate became the most important ruling body in Rome. The citizens' Assembly never had as much power as, for example, that in Athens at the time of Pericles. Even so, Romans always remembered the basic principle of their republic—that the authority of all rulers depended upon the consent of the people as a whole. For this reason, the government of Rome is summed up in the words *Senatus Populus-Que Romanus* (S.P.Q.R. for short) which means 'the Senate and People of Rome'. The letters S.P.Q.R. are found on Roman coins and on the battle standards carried by their soldiers.

Patricians and plebeians
The people did not all have an equal say in the running of their city. From early times there were two quite distinct classes in Rome—

Coin with the inscription S.P.Q.R.

the *patricians,* or nobles, and the *plebeians* (common people). The plebeians were the more recent arrivals in the city. They were mostly peasant farmers, or merchants and craftsmen. The patricians, on the other hand, were the descendants of the original founders of the city. They owned the largest estates and had the best herds of cattle and sheep. Even though they were greatly outnumbered by the plebeians, the wealthy patrician families kept many privileges for themselves. They had more votes in the Assembly than all the plebeians put together. Only members of patrician families were allowed to become magistrates, and therefore senators as well. If a plebeian owed money to a patrician and was unable to pay he could be made a slave until he had worked off his debt.

As plebeians were not allowed to marry patricians, there seemed to be no way of breaking down the barriers between the classes. Not surprisingly, the common people decided to protest about the unfairness of their position. We are told that in 494 B.C. they walked out of Rome and threatened to start a rival plebeian city nearby. This alarmed the patricians, because they could not possibly manage on their own. To get the plebeians to return they had to give way to some of their demands.

It was agreed that in future the plebeians could choose from among themselves two magistrates called *tribunes* (the number was later raised to ten). These tribunes, who held office for one year, protected the ordinary people against unfair treatment. They could not give orders or make laws, but they could veto the action of any citizen or magistrate—even a consul. This gave them great power. They were able to stop any law from being passed and could even save a man under sentence of death.

In the next 200 years or so the patricians were forced to give up their privileges one by one. Perhaps the plebeians' greatest complaint was that the laws of the city were kept secret by the magistrates and officials. This allowed dishonest patricians to take advantage of them. However, around 450 B.C., the chief laws were written down, on twelve bronze tablets, and set up in the *Forum* (market place). Penalties were fixed for each crime, most of them based upon the old principle of 'an eye for an eye, a tooth for a tooth'. For example, one said: 'If a man breaks another man's leg, and fails to give him compensation, he must lose his own leg.' This reminds us of Hammurabi's laws (see Chapter 7).

Before long, the common people were allowed to become magistrates and sit in the Senate. Then, in 367 B.C., the first plebeian was elected consul. From then on, it was agreed that one consul at least should be a plebeian. Finally, men and women from different classes were allowed to marry. This, more than anything else, reduced the differences between the nobles and the rest. But they could never be completely equal. While ordinary citizens were busy earning a living, the rich, with slaves and servants to work for them, had plenty of time to take an active part in the government. It was always very difficult for a man from a poor family to become a senior magistrate.

Under the laws of Rome no one could be buried inside the City walls. Here is the tomb of a nobleman's daughter beside the Appian Way (the main road south from the City)

34 The Conquest of Italy

In the early days of the republic the Romans had no desire to become conquerors. They simply wanted peace so that they could get on with their farming and trading. But tribes from the hills and mountains were attracted by the fertile soil and the more pleasant climate in the valley of the Tiber. They frequently raided the Latin peoples in the hope of seizing some land or stealing animals and crops. The Romans were forced to fight in order to protect their possessions. As we shall see, they soon discovered that attack was the best method of defence.

There was no regular army in the early republic. At the request of the consuls, men had to leave the land and bring their own weapons —usually spears and swords. Wealthy citizens made up the cavalry, for they alone could afford to keep horses. At first, none of the soldiers were paid. Wars were very short, mainly because both sides were eager to get back to their work. Most battles were fought in the summer; between the corn harvest of June and the grape harvest in the autumn. However, as the Roman state grew in size, special taxes were collected to provide pay for the soldiers. Men could now afford to fight longer campaigns and to receive some military training. Even so, the army was still dissolved when each war was over.

Wars against the Etruscans, Gauls and Samnites

Although the Romans had freed themselves from Etruscan rule, their neighbours across the river continued to be a serious threat. During the fifth century B.C. there were frequent wars between the Etruscans and the Latin cities under the leadership of Rome. The turning point came in 396 B.C., when the Romans captured Veii after a long seige. From then on the other Etruscan towns fell one by one and their inhabitants became subjects of Rome.

Meanwhile, far more dangerous enemies were moving down from the north. They were Gauls—tall, fair-haired people from central Europe, who had recently settled in the country we call France and just across the Alps in the valley of the river Po. The Gauls were a warlike race. In 391 B.C. a large force of them advanced through Etruria towards Rome. An army was sent to meet them, but it was heavily defeated on the banks of the River Allia (a tributary of the Tiber) only six miles from Rome. In the next year the invaders entered the city and began to burn and ransack it. Most of the population fled in terror, but a small armed force stayed behind to defend the fortress on the Capitol Hill.

In later years the Romans told a story of how one night a party of Gauls crept up the hill and started to climb the fortress walls. In a temple close at hand there was a flock of geese, sacred to a goddess called Juno. As the Gauls prepared to attack, a loud cackling was heard. The defenders awoke just in time to drive the enemy back from the walls.

We are not sure how the siege of the Capitol ended. However it appears that the Romans finally bribed the Gauls to go away by offering them a large amount of gold. Satisfied with this, they returned to the wide plain between the Alps and the Apennines which the Romans called Cisalpine Gaul (Gaul on our side of the Alps).

The conquest of Italy

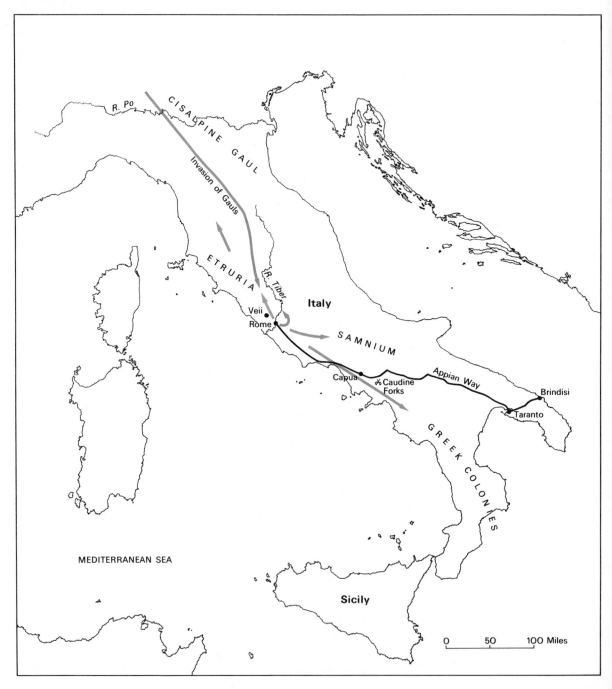

Roman expansion

Part of a triumphal arch showing Gauls bound in chains. The Romans liked to celebrate victories over their barbarian enemies

Rome was rebuilt, but all the written records of the city had been destroyed. As a result we are unsure of much of its history before 390 B.C.

Living in the mountains of central Italy were people just as tough and warlike as the Gauls. They were the Samnites, by now the only Italian tribe that was not an ally of Rome. Starting in 343 B.C. the Romans fought three long and difficult wars against the Samnites. At one time they looked like being defeated. In a narrow pass called the Caudine Forks the Roman army was trapped and forced to surrender (321 B.C.). But whenever they suffered setbacks like this the Romans showed their greatest fighting spirit. They quickly gathered fresh soldiers and hit back at the enemy. By 290 B.C. the Samnites had been conquered. They became allies of Rome, although they remained self-governing.

The challenge from Greece

The rich Greek cities along the southern coasts of Italy were alarmed by the rapid spread of Roman power. In 282 B.C. the Greeks of Taranto picked a quarrel with Rome and called to their assistance a famous Greek general called Pyrrhus. For the first time the Romans faced soldiers from overseas. Their own army was, by now, trained and well organised, but it did not seem to be any match for the army of Pyrrhus. The Greek general had 25,000 men equipped with the best weapons, twenty elephants and a much stronger cavalry.

But what the Romans lacked in equipment they made up for in courage and the strictest discipline. If any man questioned an order he was flogged. If a company of soldiers failed to stand up to the enemy it was *decimated* (one man in ten was executed). Under these conditions it is not surprising that the Romans fought like tigers. Although Pyrrhus won the first battle his losses were so heavy that he is reported to have said, 'A few more victories like this and I will be ruined'. We still speak of a 'Pyrrhic victory' when it harms the winning side more than the losers.

In 275 B.C. Pyrrhus gave up the struggle and returned to his homeland. The Greek colonies in Italy were forced to accept Roman control, and garrisons of soldiers were established in Taranto and other cities. Rome was now master of all Italy south of the river Po.

Wise government and good roads

In past ages, people who won wars against their neighbours usually helped themselves to land, cattle, crops and anything else of value they could lay hands on. They often made slaves of the people they had conquered. But as a rule the Romans did not behave in this way. They treated former enemies fairly, sometimes even generously, in the hope of making them friendly allies for the future. Thus the peoples of Italy were allowed to live in peace and manage their own affairs, as long as they paid taxes to Rome and supplied men for its army.

Gradually the privileges of Roman citizens were granted to the subject peoples, beginning with the nearby Latin cities. When a man became a full citizen, no matter where he lived he could go to Rome to help elect the magistrates and make laws in the Assembly. The Romans soon gained a reputation for justice and good government. Although they did not force their way of life on others, it was not long before Roman language, law and religion were spreading freely throughout Italy.

To join up the new settlements and to make it easier to move soldiers from place to place, a network of fine, straight roads was built throughout Italy. The most famous of these was the Appian Way, which ran 234 miles south-east from Rome. As well as soldiers on the march, the usual traffic on roads like this included chariots, covered wagons, four-wheeled carriages and farmers' carts. On horseback it was possible to cover up to 100 miles a day.

Although the Romans had no machines for earth-moving, their methods of roadbuilding were similar to those we use today. A deep trench was dug in the soil and filled with foundations—mainly layers of cobble stones, crushed rubble and concrete. The finishing touch was a cambered (curved) surface of large paving stones, carefully fitted together. Drainage ditches were cut along the roadside, and in the towns a kerb separated the highway from the pedestrians' footpath. There were milestones at intervals of one Roman mile (about 1,620 yards) marking the distance to Rome and the nearest towns. These roads were so well made that many of them still provide the basis for modern highways.

The Appian Way as it is today. Notice cobblestones from the original road

35 The Struggle with Carthage

Nearly 400 miles south of Rome, where the African coast juts out into the sea, lay the great city of Carthage. It was founded about 850 B.C. by the Phoenicians, seafaring people from the shores of the eastern Mediterranean. Its fine harbour and its central position in the Mediterranean made it an ideal trading city. Merchants from Carthage appeared in all the ports of the civilised world. They also established colonies and trading posts along the coasts of Spain, North Africa, Sardinia and western Sicily.

Colonies and trade of Carthage

Carthaginian ships carried valuable goods like silver from Spain, silk and perfumes from the East, papyrus from Egypt and even tin

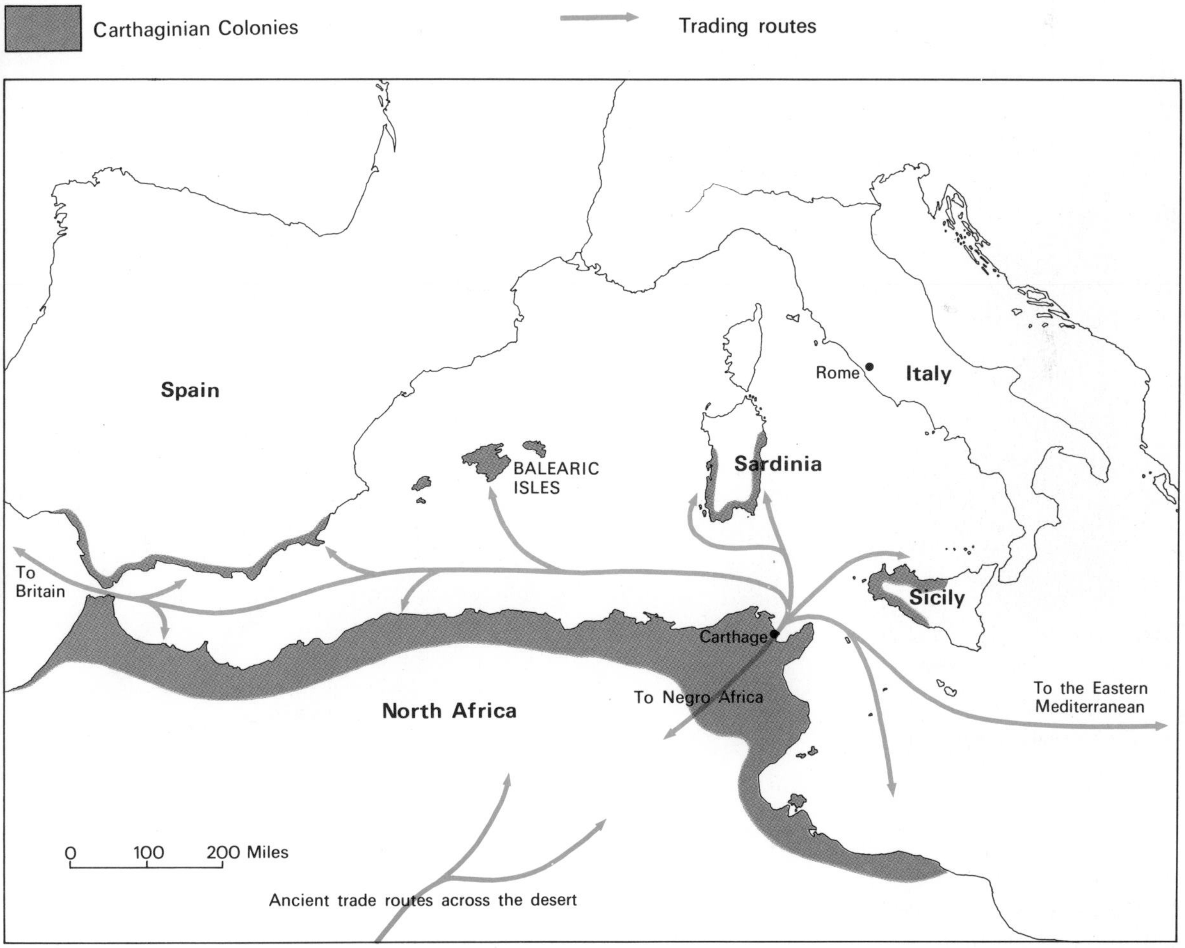
Carthaginian Colonies
Trading routes
Spain
BALEARIC ISLES
Sardinia
Rome
Italy
Sicily
Carthage
To Britain
To Negro Africa
To the Eastern Mediterranean
North Africa
0 100 200 Miles
Ancient trade routes across the desert

A Roman warship. The
crocodile is to show that
the ship had been on duty
in Egypt

from far-away Britain. These were sold or exchanged for corn, wine, olive oil, cloth and jewellery. The Carthaginians also traded with some of the Negro peoples beyond the Sahara desert. Gold, ivory, slaves, hides and ostrich feathers were carried overland and sold to the Mediterranean peoples.

Carthage was a republic, like Rome. But its government was really controlled by a small group of rich and powerful merchants. They were determined to increase trade at all costs, with the result that they often led Carthage into disputes and wars with other cities. Whenever this happened foreign soldiers were hired to fight for Carthage, because its population was too small to provide a complete army. With their great fleet of warships, the Carthaginians were capable of crushing most opposition. But they finally met their match in the third century B.C. when they went to war with Rome.

Turning forests into a fleet

For some time Roman merchants had been trying to trade in the western Mediterranean. But the Carthaginians treated them like pirates, sometimes sinking their vessels by ramming them. When the two cities became involved in a quarrel in Sicily (264 B.C.) the time had come for a showdown.

The Romans realised that to win the war they would have to gain mastery of the sea. This was easier said than done, for they had no navy and little knowledge of shipbuilding. Yet with their usual determination the Romans began to cut down whole forests and build ships in great numbers. A Carthaginian vessel that had been wrecked on the coast of Italy was used as a model. But the Romans also had ideas of their own. Standing upright against the mast of each ship was a wooden 'drawbridge' with an iron spike on the end. This looked like a bird's beak and was called a *corvus* (the Latin word for crow). When an enemy vessel came close, the drawbridge was dropped so that the spike sank into its deck and locked the two ships together. This provided a gangway for soldiers to cross and force the enemy to fight hand-to-hand. Although the Carthaginians were much better sailors, the Romans found they could defeat them in this kind of 'land battle at sea'.

Nevertheless it was a hard struggle. When the Romans landed soldiers in North Africa they were surprisingly beaten (255 B.C.). Worse still, the Roman fleet had to be rebuilt after being almost wiped out in severe storms. The war dragged on for more than twenty years, until the Romans gained the upper hand with a great naval victory off the west coast of Sicily (241 B.C.). As part of the peace agreement they took over Sicily and forced Carthage to pay a vast sum of money.

The Romans did not treat the Sicilians in the same way as the Italian peoples. They seized most of their land and made them pay heavy taxes. The island became a *province* of Rome, governed by a Roman magistrate. In 238 B.C. Sardinia and Corsica were also turned into Roman provinces. Shortly after that, following an invasion by the Gauls, the Roman army marched north and occupied Cisalpine Gaul. Their control over Italy now reached right up to the Alps.

Hannibal

Meanwhile the Carthaginians, still rich and powerful, were determined to gain revenge on Rome. Hamilcar, their leading general, built a new empire in Spain, where Carthage already had many trading posts. Spain was rich in silver mines and its people could be made into excellent soldiers. Hamilcar's hatred of Rome was so strong that he made his son Hannibal swear an oath that he would never be a friend of the Roman people.

After his father's death, Hannibal became an army general at the age of twenty-six. When a fresh war broke out with Rome he was ready with a daring scheme. Realising the enemy controlled the sea routes, Hannibal planned to march his army out of Spain, along the south coast of France and into Italy from the north. In the spring of 218 B.C., he set out, with nearly 100,000 soldiers and three dozen elephants. By mid-summer, when Hannibal crossed the wide waters of the River Rhône, his troops numbered only 60,000. Yet the worst stage of the journey lay ahead—the crossing of the Alps. The mountain passes were narrow and strewn with boulders. As winter drew nearer the ground froze and there were frequent blizzards of snow. Thousands of men and animals fell to their deaths or perished from cold and hunger.

When Hannibal finally reached the plains of northern Italy only 26,000 men had survived the march. He hoped to make up for his losses by winning the support of the Italian cities, but only the recently conquered Gauls joined him. The peoples of central Italy stayed loyal to Rome. They had no reason to help a foreign army conquer their country.

Hannibal was short of men and supplies, yet he defeated the Romans and their allies on the shores of Lake Trasimene (217 B.C.). Worse was in store for them in the next year when the two sides met at Cannae. Hannibal ordered the centre of his army to retreat. Then, when most of the Roman soldiers were hemmed in on three sides, he attacked and wiped out 70,000 men. Hannibal's losses were only 6,000!

Fortunately for the Romans Hannibal was unable to follow up his victory. The Carthaginian army was too small to attack Rome itself, even though it marched to within sight of the city. Hannibal's requests for fresh forces and supplies were ignored by his government. All he could do was establish a base in southern Italy, where he remained for another thirteen years. His last hope was that his brother, Hasdrubal, would reach him with reinforcements from Spain. But Hasdrubal was defeated and killed in 207 B.C. It is said that the news first reached Hannibal when his brother's head was thrown into the Carthaginian camp!

The Romans were now ready to move on to the attack. After conquering the Carthaginian colonies in Spain, the Roman general Scipio invaded North Africa. Hannibal was recalled to defend his homeland, and in 202 B.C. a decisive battle was fought at Zama. Hannibal's new recruits were no match for Scipio's well-trained army, which won a complete victory. Hannibal later fled to the East, where he was hunted for many years until he poisoned himself to escape capture.

A coin minted in Spain shows one of Hannibal's elephants

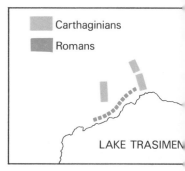

Plan of the Battle of Trasimene

Meanwhile, a peace treaty was signed (201 B.C.). Carthage had to pay a vast sum of money to Rome and give up its remaining colonies. Spain became a Roman province. The Carthaginian army was disbanded and almost all its warships destroyed. Five hundred of them were set on fire in the harbour.

Rome was now master of the western Mediterranean. Yet Carthage remained a prosperous trading city. Many Romans feared that it would recover its power. One of them was Marcus Cato, a leading figure in the Senate, who always finished his speeches with the words 'Carthage must be destroyed'. He finally got his way when Rome attacked Carthage in 149 B.C. The third Carthaginian War was little more than a bitter siege of the city, lasting three years. At the end of it, Carthage was burned to the ground and its people killed or made slaves. The conquerors ploughed up the land where the city had stood. North Africa became yet another Roman province.

The Second
Carthaginian War

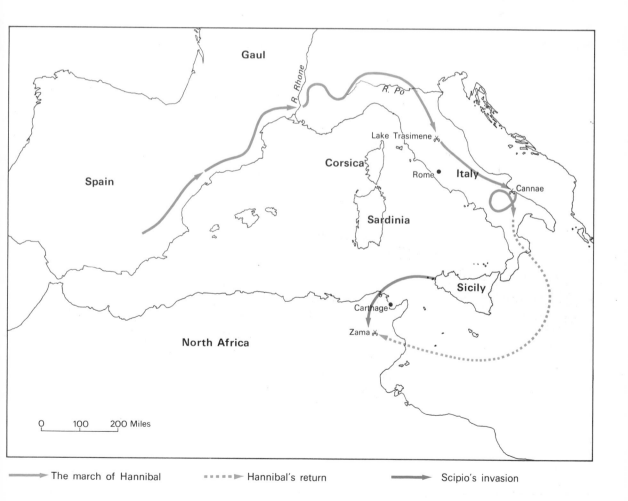

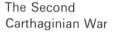

36 'Bread and Games'

Victories over Carthage gave Rome a taste for power and a desire for further conquests. Between the second and third Carthaginian Wars, Roman armies fought many battles against the rich kingdoms of the eastern Mediterranean—lands where Alexander the Great once ruled. In the space of only seventy years after the defeat of Hannibal, Macedonia, Greece and Asia Minor came under Roman rule; and Egypt was tied to Rome in a treaty of friendship. By 121 B.C. most of the rulers of lands bordering the Mediterranean had either been defeated in battle or had chosen to become allies of Rome.

Governing the provinces

In 'friendly' countries, like Egypt, the old rulers were allowed to stay in power, as long as they paid taxes and sent soldiers to help Rome. But the conquered areas were divided into provinces, under Roman governors. These men were appointed by the Senate and were changed every year. They had previously been magistrates in

The Roman Empire in 121 B.C.

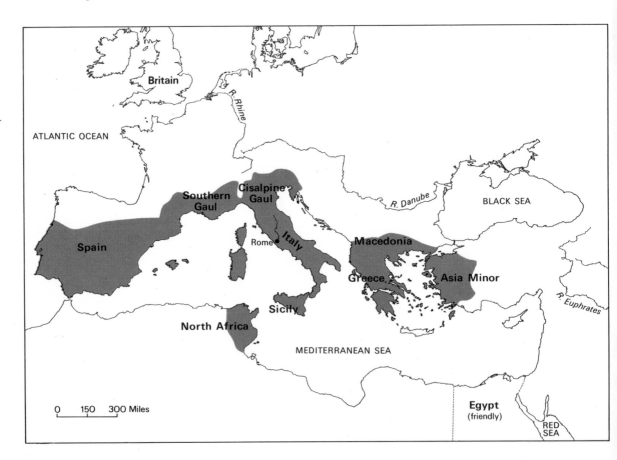

Rome. Thus a consul one year might become governor of North Africa or Macedonia the next. Perhaps the best known of all Roman governors is Pontius Pilate, who was in charge of Judaea, in Palestine, at the time of Christ's crucifixion.

Governors commanded the troops in their province and were responsible for law and order and the collection of taxes. They were officially under the control of the Senate, but Rome was far away so it was easy for them to act as though they were kings. Most governors set out to make a fortune for themselves. This was usually done through the normal system of taxing the people. Businessmen called *publicans* were employed to collect what was due to Rome plus a small profit for themselves. The governor was supposed to prevent swindling. But instead he might encourage the publicans to collect as much as they could—provided some of the extra money found its way into his pocket.

Yet generally speaking the Romans ruled fairly, allowing most of their subjects to keep their old laws, customs and religion. In less civilised provinces, like Spain or Cisalpine Gaul, the people were eager to copy Roman ways. They learned Latin, wore Roman clothes and took Roman names. Sometimes the influence was in the other direction. For example the Greeks were more advanced than the Romans themselves. Greek sculpture, painting and literature was admired and copied by educated Romans, who now learned Greek as a second language.

The rich get richer

In the early years of the republic few Roman citizens had been very rich or very poor. But foreign wars upset the old pattern of life. Some gained great wealth from the provinces; others were ruined.

Those in command of the armies came home with piles of money and valuables taken from conquered cities. One Roman was said to have brought back from Macedonia 250 wagon-loads of statues and paintings. Merchants' warehouses were filled with high-priced goods from Africa, Greece and Asia Minor. Not to be outdone, senators and magistrates filled their pockets with money from the provinces they were appointed to govern.

On the other hand, peasant farmers all over Italy suffered great hardship. They returned from fighting in the army to find their families in debt and their farms neglected. Worse still, they could no longer make a decent living out of their land. Merchants had begun to buy vast quantities of corn from Sicily and North Africa, where it could be produced much more cheaply than in Italy. There was little the peasants could do but sell their land to wealthy senators and businessmen, who grouped small farms together and turned them into sheep and cattle ranches. Meat still had to be produced near at hand and there was always a good sale for wool and leather.

These large farms, in both Italy and the provinces, were worked by slaves. They were mostly prisoners-of-war, sold in public slave markets all over Italy. Their masters treated them harshly, often putting them in chains to prevent escape. They were also underfed,

Greek sculptures, like this one of a discus thrower, were admired and copied by the Romans. The athlete on page 85 is also a Roman copy of a Greek original statue

scantily clothed, flogged regularly and sometimes forced to sleep in smelly underground barracks.

As family farms disappeared thousands of homeless peasants drifted to Rome. Few found work, for there were no large industries in those days. They merely swelled the numbers of idle citizens already crowding the slums in the low-lying parts of the city.

These unfortunate people were kept from starving by handouts of free corn, wine and olive oil. Wealthy Romans who wished to be elected to some important office had to please the 'mob' in order to get their votes. This they did with 'bread and games'—giving away food and organising free entertainments like fights between *gladiators* (armed professional fighters). You can read about later Roman 'games' in Chapter 39.

The people versus the Senate

Only the wealthiest citizens could afford to buy popularity with 'bread and games'. As a result most important positions in the government were filled by men from a few rich families. The Senate, which contained ex-magistrates, had almost complete control of

A Roman mosaic showing slaves working on an estate

Rome's affairs. This was all very well so long as the senators governed according to the wishes of the people. But this did not happen. Once they were elected, wealthy magistrates and senators forgot all about the 'mob' who had supported them and looked after the selfish interests of their own class.

The common people became very discontented, and their tribunes had terrible quarrels with the Senate. In 133 B.C. a tribune called Tiberius Gracchus put forward a plan to help the unemployed. He suggested that the great estates of the rich should be broken up and most of the land used for resettling peasant farmers. But he met violent opposition from the great landowners. They stirred up riots in which Gracchus and many of his followers were killed.

Ten years later Tiberius's brother Gaius also became a tribune. His answer to the problem of unemployment was to set up special 'colonies' for peasants, in southern Italy and North Africa. But these schemes collapsed when Gaius, like his brother, met a violent death in a riot started by leading senators. For the first time fighting had broken out within the walls of Rome. Such violence was to be repeated many times during the next hundred years.

Tiberius and Gaius Gracchus lost their fight against the selfish rule of the Senate. But the common people soon found other leaders who opposed the wealthy ruling families. Popular generals, supported by their soldiers, began to take sides in the struggle for power. The outcome was civil war, lasting on and off for nearly a century. When it was over the old republican government had been swept away and Rome began to be ruled by a line of emperors.

Troubled times

In 107 B.C. the people chose a peasant's son called Marius to be consul. It was very unusual for a man from a humble home to reach such a high position. But Marius was a good soldier, and he promised to finish a war which had been dragging on for some time in Numidia (North Africa). The generals chosen by the Senate had been failures, yet Marius soon crushed the enemy.

When he returned to Rome Marius was the hero of the people. They made him consul five times running (104–100 B.C.) even though it was one of the oldest rules of the republic that ten years must go by before a consul could be re-elected. The main reason for

javelin

helmet

jerkin

sword

shield

Roman legionary. Notice—Iron helmet; jerkin (strengthened with strips of metal); curved shield (made of hide rimmed with iron); short, double-edged stabbing sword; metal-tipped javelin (usually two). Javelins were thrown while approaching the enemy (up to a distance of 40 yards) and swords were used at close quarters. On the march, legionaries wore hobnailed boots and carried a heavy pack with rations, clothes, cooking pot and other equipment. They were expected to march twenty miles or more a day and build a fortified camp each evening keeping Marius in power was to allow him to deal with a new danger that had arisen in the north. Hundreds of thousands of German tribesmen had invaded Gaul and were threatening the frontiers of Italy itself.

On his previous campaign, Marius had thoroughly re-organised the army. Instead of calling up ordinary citizens, who disliked fighting long wars on foreign soil, he raised volunteers who were willing to make the army a full-time career. From now on soldiers enlisted for at least sixteen years. Marius divided each *legion* (regiment) into ten *cohorts* of up to 600 men. Cohorts were made up of six *centuries*, each containing a maximum of 100 troops. These were commanded, as before, by *centurions* — experienced soldiers usually promoted from the ranks. The foot soldiers were normally Italians, but cavalry, archers and others were mostly drawn from the provinces.

With his highly trained, professional army Marius won two great victories against the German tribes (102–101 B.C.). Rome was safe and Marius returned to lead the common people in opposition to the Senate. But he was not as good a statesman as he was a general. His supporters soon lost faith in him and he left the country.

Marius had made his soldiers take an oath of obedience not to Rome but to him personally. Other commanders followed his example, so it was now possible for a successful general to rule Rome by force. Sulla, a rich nobleman and a bitter opponent of Marius, saw his chance. In 88 B.C. he marched into Rome with his army. After killing many of his opponents, he took away the powers of the people's Assembly and the tribunes and made the Senate once more the ruling body. But these changes did not last. The Senate had lost its authority over the people and could not control the generals. When Sulla died (78 B.C.) the government was weaker than ever.

Meanwhile disturbances all over the Empire threatened to bring about its collapse. There were revolts in Spain and Asia Minor, and the Mediterranean was swarming with pirates who robbed shipping and raided coastal towns. Earlier, in 91 B.C., the subject peoples of Italy had risen in rebellion against Rome. They complained that although they provided most of the soldiers for the army few of them had the privileges of Roman citizens. After two years of civil war they were defeated by Roman troops under Sulla. But their demands were granted soon afterwards, when all free men in Italy were made Roman citizens.

The peace in Italy was again broken (73 B.C.) by a serious slave revolt in the south. It began in Capua, at a 'combat school', where slaves were trained to fight in the arena. Led by a gladiator called Spartacus, a group of skilled swordsmen made a daring escape. Thousands of slaves from the great ranches ran away to join them. Before long a vast slave army was roaming the countryside, robbing and burning the houses of landlords. It seemed that the capital itself was in danger. But the rebels were finally overcome by an army under Marcus Crassus, one of the richest men in Rome. In bitter revenge 6,000 prisoners were crucified along the Appian Way (71 B.C.).

Crassus got his reward when he was elected consul in the following year. The other consul was a popular young officer named Pompey, who was soon to become the most powerful man in Rome.

Pompey and Caesar

In 67 B.C. Pompey was given the task of clearing the pirates from the Mediterranean. With 200 warships it took him only three months to chase them from the seas and destroy their bases. In the next year Pompey left Rome at the head of a large army, with instructions to win back Asia Minor, which had rebelled against Rome. After a brilliant campaign not only Asia Minor but also Syria and Palestine were brought firmly under Roman rule.

When Pompey came home after five years in the East he was awarded the highest honours. The Senate granted him a *Triumph*, the ambition of every general. This was a great procession from the gates of Rome to the Capitol Hill. Senators and magistrates led the way, followed by prisoners of war and the victorious army with its general seated in a chariot and wearing a laurel wreath on his head. The ceremony ended with a sacrifice at the temple of Jupiter, King of the Gods.

Many people expected Pompey to overthrow the Senate and make himself ruler of Rome. But he hesitated, probably deciding that the time was not ripe. In any case he had some powerful rivals, including

Pompey

Gladiators fighting

Crassus and a wealthy nobleman who had gained importance as a leader of the common people. His name was Gaius Julius Caesar.

Caesar realised that the Empire needed a new kind of government under *one* ruler who was both a soldier and a statesman. He longed to be that man. Once, when passing through a village in the Alps, he said to his companions: 'I would rather be head of this tiny village than second in command in Rome'. Caesar knew that the only way to achieve his ambition was to get control of an army and become a famous conqueror like Pompey. His chance came in 58 B.C., when he was made governor of the two provinces in Gaul; one north of Italy (Cisalpine Gaul) and the other along the south coast of France.

The northern part of Gaul was outside the Empire. This did not satisfy Caesar. In the next nine years he gradually conquered the whole of the country, advancing the frontier to the North Sea and the river Rhine. He even found time to make two expeditions to Britain, although he did not stay long enough to establish Roman rule (see Chapter 45). We can still read Caesar's own account of his campaigns, in which he described the people he conquered.

Caesar had gained a whole new province for Rome and had shown himself to be a great general. He planned each campaign skilfully and shared every hardship and danger with his troops. Not only were his soldiers devoted to him; he was also the hero of the common people of Rome. It seemed only Pompey could stop him taking over

Caesar in armour

the government when he returned from Gaul (Crassus was killed on a campaign in the East, 53 B.C.).

Jealous of Caesar's popularity, Pompey grew more friendly with the Senate. When Caesar set out for Rome (49 B.C.) the Senate instructed him to disband his army. But the order was ignored, so Pompey and the leading senators fled to Greece to raise troops. Caesar took charge of the capital, where he was given a great welcome. Early in the following year he caught up with his enemies in northern Greece and defeated them at Pharsalus. Pompey escaped to Egypt, where he was murdered.

After finishing off all remaining opposition, Caesar returned to Rome in 45 B.C. He was now master of the Mediterranean world.

Roman soldiers in action: they have formed what was called a *tortoise* with their locked shields and are attacking a defended position

38 'The Second Founder of Rome'

Caesar had not been elected by the people, but most of them welcomed him as their ruler. The soldiers called him *Imperator* (commander-in-chief). From this we get the word *emperor*, meaning a king who rules an empire, or group of countries. Caesar did not actually take the title of king, but he was a king in all but name. He controlled the appointment of magistrates and took away most of the powers of the Senate.

Caesar's brief rule

The new master of Rome showed that he was a wise ruler as well as a great general. He improved the government of the provinces, making methods of tax collection fairer. He tried to help unemployed Romans by setting up new colonies in the provinces where they could buy land cheaply and settle down to farm it. Work was also provided by new schemes to rebuild the centre of Rome and construct more roads in Italy. Through these efforts, Caesar more than halved the number of citizens receiving free bread.

Today he is perhaps best remembered for the changes he made in the Roman calendar. At that time its twelve months were measured by the moon; making 355 days in a year. As a result the months gradually got in front of the seasons. Caesar ordered that in future Romans would use the Egyptian Solar (Sun) calendar of 365 days with a leap year every fourth year (see Chapter 3). He renamed the seventh month Julius (now July) after his own name. Augustus, the next ruler of Rome, called the eighth month August.

Caesar planned many more reforms, but he did not live to carry them out. On 15 March 44 B.C. he was brutally stabbed to death in the Senate House by a group of senators. Some of them, including Gaius Cassius, were jealous of his power. Others, like Marcus Brutus, believed they were doing the right thing for Rome. They hated the way Caesar was adored like a god. When statues of him began to appear in the temples they feared his next step would be to make himself king. If this happened, and members of his family became kings after him, the people would never again be free to choose their rulers.

This coin was struck by Brutus and the conspirators after the murder of Caesar. It shows a cap and daggers standing for liberty, and the words *Ides of March* (the date, half way through the month)

Antony and Octavian

Caesar's murderers hoped to see a return of the republic, but they were mistaken. Control of the Roman armies passed to followers of Caesar—particularly Mark Antony, his close friend, and Octavian, his great-nephew and adopted son. At the time of the murder Octavian was only eighteen and finishing his education in Greece.

In a clever speech at Caesar's funeral Antony turned the people against the murderers. Then, joining Octavian, he defeated them at

Philippi in Macedonia (42 B.C.). Brutus and Cassius killed themselves to avoid being captured.

Having revenged Caesar's death, Antony and Octavian divided the Empire between them. Octavian controlled the West. He had none of the brilliance of Caesar but he was firm and sensible and he learned to govern wisely. Antony, who ruled the East, was a tough and experienced soldier. But he soon fell in love with Cleopatra, the Queen of Egypt, and led a life of luxury and idleness in her royal court. Octavian grew angry with him for neglecting his duties. A complete break between them came in 33 B.C., when Antony

The altar of peace built by Augustus in memory of himself. An example of the fine stone architecture from his reign

divorced his wife (Octavian's sister) in order to marry Cleopatra.

Octavian declared war. In 31 B.C. the rival fleets met in a great sea battle near Actium, on the west coast of Greece. The result was still in doubt when Cleopatra foolishly ordered her ships to retreat. Antony followed her and the battle was lost. Octavian hurried after the lovers, to Egypt, where they both committed suicide.

The Emperor 'Augustus'

Egypt became a new Roman province and Octavian returned home as sole ruler of the Empire. Like Caesar, his position depended on the support of the army. In fact, from now on it was necessary for every ruler of Rome to be hailed as Imperator by his soldiers.

Octavian wanted the ordinary people to trust him as well. Instead of sweeping away the old traditions, as Caesar had done, he pretended to bring back the republic. The Senate continued to meet and the Assembly elected magistrates and passed laws. But Octavian made sure nothing was done without his approval. He always had the right of speaking first in the Senate so that the senators knew what he wanted! At the same time he was consul, tribune, chief priest and *princeps* (first citizen), although he was usually known simply as *Augustus*, meaning 'His Majesty'.

Augustus ruled for well over forty years, until his death in A.D. 14. He is often called 'the Second Founder of Rome', for it was he who brought the civil wars to an end and established the rule of emperors which lasted for nearly 500 years.

Augustus gave people in the provinces honest and capable governors. Unlike Caesar he did not try to add new lands to the Empire. Rome already ruled a vast territory, from the Atlantic in the west to the Euphrates in the east; from the Rhine in the north to the Sahara in the south. Augustus decided this was enough. He disbanded more than half the sixty legions at his command and stationed the rest in camps guarding the frontiers. His policy of peace and order greatly helped trade. So did the new roads he built, linking the provinces with each other and with Rome.

In the capital Augustus kept the poor in a good mood, giving them free food, amusements and occasional gifts of money. He established a police force and fire brigade and made sure the streets were kept clean. So many fine temples and public buildings were put up that it was said 'Augustus found Rome made of brick and left it made of marble'.

Augustus dressed as a Roman senator

A stone carving showing lions drinking

39 The Roman Peace

For about 200 years, starting with the reign of Augustus, there was peace throughout the Empire. In this time Roman civilisation spread far and wide. The provinces enjoyed greater safety and prosperity than ever before. It was such a change from all the wars of the past that this period became famous for the *Pax Romana* (Roman Peace).

For half a century there was a kind of 'royal family', as each of the first four emperors after Augustus was related to him. They were all peculiar in some way. For example Caligula made his horse a consul and built a special palace for him! Claudius, who came next, was physically deformed and spoke with a stammer. But he was wiser than he looked. The last of the four, Nero (A.D. 54–68), was cruel, wasteful and quick to murder anyone who stood in his way. Nero loved to show off. He acted in the theatre and sang or recited his poems in public. On one occasion he joined the gladiators in the arena and killed a lion with a club. But this was not the kind of behaviour expected of a ruler. The soldiers and the people finally turned against him and he committed suicide.

The Roman Empire in A.D. 117

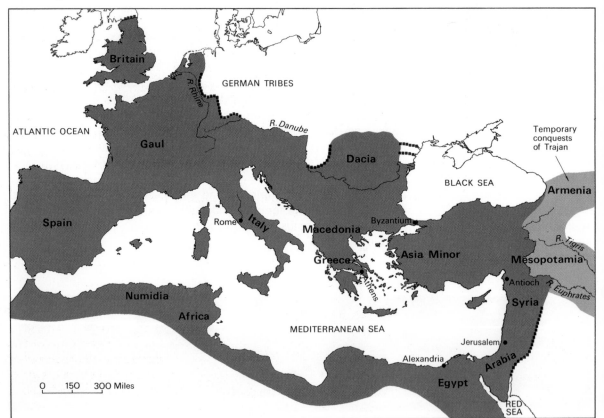

 Main walls and fortifications

After Nero the Empire was usually ruled by a popular general. Some were dangerous lunatics, others were strong and wise. From A.D. 96–180 there was an unbroken line of good emperors. Although none of them were related, each had become the adopted son of the previous ruler.

Guarding the frontier

Augustus hoped to achieve lasting peace by keeping the Empire within its existing boundaries. He stationed his largest army on the banks of the Rhine, to keep back the restless German tribes. But the emperor Trajan (A.D. 98–117) was more adventurous. Roman defences along the Danube were threatened by wandering Asian tribes, so he took an army across the river and occupied Dacia (present-day Rumania). He also extended the Empire in the East (Armenia and Mesopotamia) but these conquests were short-lived.

Hadrian, who followed Trajan as emperor, spent fifteen years travelling around the Empire and strengthening its defences. He attempted no further conquests. Instead he built walls, ditches and forts along the whole northern frontier. By this time Britain was a Roman province. We can still see remains of the great wall Hadrian built between the river Tyne and the Solway Firth.

Army camps along the frontiers grew into permanent settlements, with their own houses, shops and baths. Soldiers married local women and when they retired they were usually given farms nearby. In time their sons often joined the same legion.

Meanwhile, inside the frontiers, peace and order helped the growth of trade. The roads were safe and the seas were free of pirates. Peace also helped the spread of civilisation in the western provinces. In Gaul, Spain and Britain walled towns grew up. Their buildings were similar to those in the capital, but, unlike Rome, the streets were planned in a chessboard pattern, crossing each other at right angles.

All the people of the provinces now thought of themselves as Romans. Some became governors, generals or even emperors – like Trajan, who was born in Spain. Finally, in A.D. 213, every freeborn subject in the Empire was made a full Roman citizen.

The busy life of the capital

Rome was by far the greatest city of the ancient world. Hundreds of thousands of people lived there, closely packed together. Such a dense population was only made possible by the excellent water supply. Several *aqueducts* (canals on long lines of arches) carried water from surrounding hillsides into the city, where it fed public taps and fountains or was piped directly into the homes of the rich.

Like all great cities Rome was full of contrasts. From the Palatine Hill, where the emperor lived in a luxurious marble palace, it was a short walk to the noisy slum district of Subura. Here the narrow streets were piled with rubbish and crowded with tradesmen, pedlars, brawling drunkards, thieves, beggars and idlers. No man who cared for his safety would go there at night, when the streets were dark.

Nero

A Roman aqueduct in France

Almost every kind of tradesman could be found in the capital. There were gold- and silver-smiths, jewellers, cutlers, clothmakers, potters, leather workers, glassmakers, stonemasons, carpenters and dozens more. Many of them made luxury goods for the rich, using materials brought from overseas. Precious metals came from provinces like Spain and Africa; glassware, papyrus and perfumes were shipped from Egypt, while far-away India and China provided silk, spices, emeralds and pearls. It is true to say that the world supplied Rome, while Rome supplied the rest of Italy.

Craftsmen usually worked in their own shops, assisted by slaves and apprentices. There were no factories, for powered machines were unheard of in ancient times. Goods were sold either from market stalls or from ordinary shops, which were opened and closed with wooden shutters. In some streets all the shops were of the same kind, for example 'the street of shoemakers'. These were useful landmarks in directing strangers about the city, for streets were rarely named and houses had no numbers.

During the morning the main centre of activity was the Forum, at the foot of the Palatine and Capitol Hills. This was the meeting place of businessmen, politicians and lawyers. The market stalls which once filled the square had been pushed into smaller forums nearby. Much of the space was now filled with law courts, temples, the Senate House and offices of merchants and bankers. The whole area was crammed with people of every race and occupation, all pushing and shoving. Marriages, funerals and religious processions crowded the streets in other parts of the city. As a result ordinary wheeled traffic was forbidden until nightfall (except for carts carrying building materials).

Most people left work during the afternoon and set out for one of the public baths. Roman baths were quite different from anything we have today. They were recreation centres where people of all classes could bathe, exercise and gossip with friends before returning home for dinner. As well as hot, cold and warm baths there were usually massage rooms. In these, bathers could have their bodies oiled and massaged by specially trained slaves. Afterwards they could relax in lounges, libraries or restaurants. There was usually a gymnasium, and also an ordinary swimming pool; the only place where mixed bathing was allowed.

While most people went to the baths, some young men preferred riding, wrestling or athletic sports on the Field of Mars, a large open space near the banks of the Tiber. Swimming in the river was also very popular.

At present most people have about 120 days' holiday every year (including weekends). In Rome roughly the same amount of time was given to public holidays and religious festivals. It was on these days that public entertainments were held. They were provided free by the State or, occasionally, by private citizens seeking popularity.

Inside the Baths of Caracalla in Rome

The Colosseum today

The biggest event was chariot racing at the Circus Maximus. This was nothing like a circus as we know it. It was a great racecourse, with places for 150,000 spectators. In each race four horse-drawn chariots covered seven laps of the course, a distance of about five miles. There was tremendous rivalry between the stables and heavy betting among the spectators. The charioteers needed great skill to take the sharp bends at each end of the arena. They wore crash helmets and padded clothing, yet there were many fatal accidents. Those that survived and were successful became rich and famous, even though they were slaves.

Actors were also slaves. They performed in large, open-air theatres similar to those of the Greeks. But as a rule the common people preferred to go to the 'games' in the *amphitheatre* (an oval-shaped arena with seats rising all round). At the Colosseum (opened in A.D. 80) up to 50,000 spectators watched all kinds of brutal and bloodthirsty entertainments. Gladiators were matched against wild beasts — lions, tigers, panthers and bears — or against each other, separately and in groups. The favourite contest was between a fast-moving man with a net and trident (three-pronged spear) and a fully armed opponent with sword and shield. When one of them was wounded and at the other's mercy the crowd decided his fate by signalling 'thumbs up' or 'thumbs down'. Hardly ever was the 'thumbs up' sign given to spare his life.

Sometimes the arena was flooded for a sea battle between rival warships. This provided plenty of killings and drownings to amuse the spectators. It is difficult for us to understand how the Romans could get such pleasure from watching suffering and death. The sight of human beings reduced to bloodstained heaps of twitching flesh seemed the only thing to make the poor forget the miseries of their own lives.

40 People and Customs

The old division between patricians and plebeians had now almost disappeared. But Romans were still divided into classes, according to wealth and position. At the top were generals, governors, magistrates and others holding important positions in government. Such men often came from families that had grown rich during the foreign wars of the republic. Next came what we would call the 'middle classes'— businessmen of all kinds, including merchants, bankers and tax collectors. Below were the ordinary craftsmen and shopkeepers; the 'city mob' (mostly idlers living on free bread) and the slaves, who were now the largest class in Rome and all Italy.

We know a great deal about the lives of wealthy and educated Romans, from their letters and diaries as well as the contents of their homes. But we have less information about the way of life of poorer people. Therefore, while reading the next three chapters, it is important to remember that those living in ease and comfort were only a small number in the total population.

Family life

Romans belonged not only to families but also to larger groups which were like Scottish clans. This can be seen in their names. It was usual to have three. The first was personal, like our Christian name. There were only a dozen or so common ones for men; including Gaius, Lucius, Marcus and Publius. Popular women's names included Cornelia, Julia and Flavia. Next came the clan name, followed by the name of the family (the branch of the clan).

A Roman father had complete control over everyone in the household. Children were brought up to obey his orders instantly and without question. Even when the sons of the family were grown up and had children of their own they still had to obey their father. This discipline and sense of duty was one of the reasons why Romans made such good soldiers.

Fathers chose husbands and wives for their children. Marriage 'for love' was rare among young people in Roman times. Many girls were married at the age of thirteen or so, and their husbands were not much older. When the wedding ceremony was over the groom pretended to snatch his bride from the arms of her mother. Then followed a procession through the streets to the home of the newly-weds. The bride was carried over the threshold, and after prayers and blessings the guests went home. The wife wore a ring on the third finger of her left hand, just as married women do today.

Once they were married Roman women enjoyed freedom and respect. The Greeks rarely allowed their wives to meet strangers. They shut them indoors and spent little time with them. But a Roman wife was her husband's close companion and helper. She

Part of a wedding
ceremony

shared his authority in the home and often went out to dinner parties
with him. Whenever he was away she took over the running of the
household.

The Romans had no labour-saving devices to make housework
easier, so those who could afford it bought slaves to do the chores.
A family had to be really poor not to own at least one household
slave. The rich had dozens of them. Trained and intelligent slaves
(often Greeks) could cost ten or twelve times more than untrained
ones. They were too valuable to be sent to work on farms or in mines
and quarries. Instead they became household servants, secretaries,
librarians, teachers and so on.

A slave was not protected by the law. There was nothing to stop
his master from working him to death, or even torturing and executing
him. Many innocent slaves were branded with red hot irons, burnt
alive, crucified or thrown to wild animals in the amphitheatre. But
although cruelty of this kind was fairly common, most owners
realised that they could get more out of their slaves if they treated

them well. Sometimes a household slave became a great favourite of the family and was finally set free as a reward for good service.

Clothes

Most Romans dressed fairly simply. Indoors, men wore a short-sleeved tunic—a kind of knee-length shirt, gathered at the waist by a belt. These were usually made of wool, although rich men often wore linen or silk tunics, embroidered with gold thread. Out of doors, men changed from sandals to leather shoes and put on a *toga.* This was a large piece of white woollen cloth, rather like a blanket, with one edge straight and the other curved. It was wound round the body, over the shoulders and under the arms.

Only Roman citizens were allowed to wear a toga. This was important in earlier times, before the Italians and others were granted citizenship. People were proud to be seen in their togas, even though they were awkward to wear and had to be taken off for any kind of hard work or exercise. Senators distinguished themselves from ordinary citizens by wearing a toga with a stripe. Cloaks of various kinds were put over the top in chilly weather, but hats were rarely worn, except on long journeys in very hot sun.

In the early years of the republic most women wore plain togas. But these were gradually replaced by coloured cloaks. Underneath they wore a linen vest, covered by a long-sleeved cotton or silk tunic, reaching to the ankles. Women liked to wear lots of jewellery—rings, bracelets, necklaces, brooches and ear-rings—and very complicated hairstyles. They sometimes grew their hair very long and piled it in coils on top of their heads. Hair dyes, wigs and false hair-pieces were commonly used. So were perfumes, cosmetics, eyebrow-tweezers, nail-files and other aids to beauty.

A man in a toga holding busts of his ancestors

An elaborate hairstyle

Much of what we know about Roman houses comes from findings at Pompeii, near Naples, and Ostia, the port at the mouth of the Tiber. In the centuries since the end of the Empire most Roman towns have been pulled down and built over. The ruins of a few, like Ostia, have been safely buried in thick layers of river mud. But the best preserved is Pompeii. On 24 August, A.D. 79, the volcano Vesuvius erupted, burying the town and most of its inhabitants under a shower of ashes and a great tide of volcanic lava.

Nearly 1,700 years passed before archaeologists began to dig out Pompeii. Gradually houses, squares and public buildings were uncovered. Among the bones of the dead and the rubble of fallen roofs lay furniture, statues, cups, plates and even remains of food on tables! These findings have greatly increased our knowledge of life in Roman times, especially of the homes people lived in.

The apartments of the poor

In the larger towns, like Rome and Ostia, only wealthy families could afford separate houses of their own. Poorer families usually rented one or two rooms in apartment houses—blocks of flats with long flights of stairs. Many of these people had no beds to sleep on. They had to make do with mats on the floor. Their only furniture was a table and benches or stools.

Flat dwellers fetched their water from the nearest public fountain. They also depended on public lavatories, although some families kept a pot under the table and emptied it out of the window after dark. It was unfortunate if anyone happened to be passing by at the time!

Windows in these houses had no glass. They were opened and closed with wooden shutters. When the weather was chilly people had to choose between a cold draught (if they opened the shutters) or darkness (if they closed them). The commonest form of lighting was an olive-oil lamp, but this was expensive. Most people preferred to go to bed early and get up before sunrise, to make full use of daylight hours.

There were no fireplaces or chimneys in apartment houses. For cooking and heating an open fire was lit in a brazier (a metal container, still used today by street workmen). This was very dangerous. If one of the tenants carelessly knocked over his fire the whole building could burn down in a few minutes.

The houses and villas of the rich

In contrast to these small, overcrowded apartments the town houses of wealthy families were roomy and comfortable. They were made of brick or stone, whitewashed on the outside to reflect the glare of the

Sundial—It was a slab of marble, divided into sections, on which an iron marker cast a shadow. The Roman day was divided into twelve equal hours which were longer in summer and shorter in winter. But the end of the sixth hour was always noon. When they went out most Romans were content to get a rough idea of the time from the position of the sun

sun. Unlike most modern houses they were usually built on one floor only and they faced inwards, away from the deafening noise of the streets. It was rare to find windows facing the street. As an extra protection against noise the front of the house, on either side of the entrance hall, was often sealed off from the living rooms and let as shops.

The entrance hall opened into a central living room called the *atrium.* This had a hole in the ceiling to let in daylight and to let out smoke from the fire. Below it was the *impluvium*, a shallow tank cut in the floor to collect rainwater. In earlier times the whole family worked, ate and slept in the atrium. Sometimes small bedrooms and storerooms opened off it, and there was usually a back garden.

Wealth gained during the foreign wars of the republic made possible large extensions to these houses. Bedrooms, studies and other rooms were built on to the atrium, which became just a reception room or lounge. The wealthiest families converted the back garden into a whole new section of the house. This was the *peristyle,* a square courtyard with a covered walk or verandah running along the sides. In the centre were flower beds, a pool or fountain and usually a sundial.

On all sides of the peristyle were additional rooms, including a kitchen, dining room, summer lounge, bathroom and toilet. Many of these houses had a kind of central heating system. This was called a *hypocaust* (hot underneath) because hot air from a furnace passed through hollow tiles below the floor (and sometimes inside the walls as well).

Romans never filled up their rooms with furniture as we do. But as houses grew larger furnishings became more luxurious. Bare stools, chairs and tables were inlaid with ivory or silver. Ordinary earthenware dishes were replaced by decorated gold and silver plate. Ornamental lampstands and small statues of bronze or marble

Apartment houses in Ostia

Plan: town house

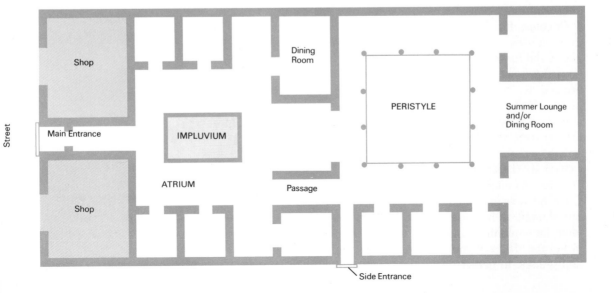

appeared; most of them brought from Greece or the eastern provinces. Pictures were painted on the walls and *mosaic* floors were laid. These were designs or pictures made up of hundreds of coloured stones set in concrete.

Priceless furnishings and decorations were found not only in the town houses of the rich but also in their *villas* (country mansions). It was usual for them to spend the summer months in their villas, away from the noise and stuffy heat of the town. They were like holiday houses, set in pleasant gardens with flower beds, fountains and fish ponds. Many villas were built near the sea or surrounded by parks and woods where deer and boar could be hunted. Hunting and fishing were the two most popular pastimes of Romans on holiday.

A rich man's house at Pompeii

Food and eating habits

Ordinary families lived mainly on bread, made from wheat or barley. Olive oil was used instead of butter, and cheese was usually made out of goats' milk. Vegetables like broad beans, lettuces and cabbages were fairly plentiful, but potatoes and tomatoes were not yet known in Europe. The commonest fruits were apples, pears, cherries, plums and grapes. In earlier times meat was usually eaten on festival days only. But before long wealthier families began to eat large quantities of it. As well as beef, mutton and pork they liked the costly meat of flamingos, peacocks and storks! Above all they loved good quality fish. Wine was drunk by all classes, for there was no tea, coffee or cocoa.

Most Romans had a light breakfast. There was always a great hurry to get to work at dawn, so a drink of wine or water and a little bread and cheese was about all they had time for. The first proper meal was at midday. It might consist of cold meat, vegetables, bread and wine, with fresh fruit to follow.

The main meal of the day was dinner, about four hours later. Wealthy families had several courses of meat or fish, with vegetables and fruit. The wine was usually warmed and diluted with about three times as much water. Slaves prepared and served the food. The stoves they used had hollows in the top filled with charcoal which was fanned into a fire beneath the cooking pots.

At one time the family sat on chairs round a table in the atrium. Later they had a separate dining room and copied Greek customs of eating. They lay on couches and helped themselves to the dishes on a low table in the middle. Spoons and knives were used but forks were unknown. Most of the eating was done with the fingers, so slaves carried napkins and finger bowls. In other ways Roman table manners were different from ours. For example, what was left of the dinner was thrown on the floor!

Sometimes friends and relations were invited to a dinner party. Unlike an ordinary family meal this might go on far into the night and there would be much more drinking. Between courses there were long and serious conversations, and special entertainments were often arranged for the guests. Slaves read poetry aloud, and there were sometimes musicians and jugglers, even acrobats or dancing girls.

A butcher's shop: you can see his scales on the right

42 Schools and Books

In the early years of the republic Romans had little interest in education. There were few schools, for most children were taught by their fathers. Apart from learning the 'Twelve Tables' of the law by heart, they did little else beyond basic reading, writing and counting. But after the conquest of Greece, in the second century B.C., Greek methods of education began to spread throughout the Empire. In the towns private schools were set up, many of them with Greek teachers.

Roman education

Children of wealthy parents were first taught at home by a private tutor (often a Greek slave). Then, at the age of about seven, boys went to an elementary school. Fees were always charged, for there were no state schools like we have today. Girls usually continued their education at home, because learning to manage a household was an important part of it.

Most elementary schools were quite small, having perhaps thirty or forty pupils and a teacher in one large room. Classes normally began before dawn and ended around noon. Therefore pupils carried lamps on their way to school. Their tutors went with them and sat at the back of the room during lessons.

At this stage most of the time was spent on reading, writing and counting. Discipline was very strict. Some teachers flogged pupils not only for disobedience but also for making the slightest mistake,

A Roman school; two older pupils are sitting on either side of the master with scrolls in their hands. A slave with a satchel stands on the right

like getting a sum wrong or misreading a word! Capital letters were learned first (almost the same as the ones we use today). After this the children learned a 'running style' of writing. Latin, unlike English, is always pronounced the way it is spelt. Therefore spelling was easily mastered. But sums were very difficult with Roman numerals. As in Greece, younger pupils counted on the beads of an *abacus* (see Chapter 28).

When they were about twelve boys went to a 'grammar school', provided their parents could afford the fees. Here they learned Greek and studied the works of great Greek and Roman writers. Most of it was poetry, for novels and adventure stories were unknown. Pupils had to write essays and compose their own poems. They were also taught some mathematics and a little history, but the main aim was to train them in *oratory* (the art of public speaking). Most of the important men in Roman life were lawyers and politicians, all of them skilful speakers. Therefore pupils had to learn and recite long passages of poetry and famous speeches, like those of Cicero, a senator in the days of Pompey and Caesar.

After the age of sixteen or so some pupils continued their education in Athens, Alexandria, or one of the other great centres of learning. But only the richest families could afford to send their sons abroad.

Books and writing

As in Greece, children learned to write with a stylus on wooden boards covered with wax. Adults also used wax boards for notes and short letters. Two or more boards could be tied together by passing a cord through holes in the edges.

Paper was still unknown in Europe. The nearest things to it were papyrus and parchment, both expensive. Papyrus was first made in ancient Egypt, but parchment came later. It was produced from the skins of animals, usually sheep and goats. Although it was heavier and stronger than papyrus it was too costly for most uses. Pointed reeds or goose feathers were used for writing on these surfaces. Their tips were split, like modern pen nibs. Ink was made by mixing various ingredients, including soot, water and resin—a gum obtained from plants.

Books were not made as they are today. Sheets of papyrus, eight to ten inches wide, were glued together to form a roll which was sometimes as long as 35 feet. This was called a *volume*, from the Latin word *volvo*, meaning 'I roll'. The volume was glued to a stick of wood or ivory, rolled tightly on to it and fastened with cord or leather thongs. The writing was done in columns, three to four inches wide. As it was read the volume was unrolled, column by column. At first parchment was used in a similar way. But by the third century A.D. it began to be cut into sheets which were sewn together and bound in a cover, like a modern book.

Needless to say, all volumes were copied by hand. Some booksellers had dozens of copy-slaves working in a separate room behind the shop. The original text was read aloud to them so that a number of copies could be produced at the same time.

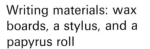

Writing materials: wax boards, a stylus, and a papyrus roll

Rich families built up large collections of volumes; but most people used public libraries. By the fourth century A.D. there were twenty-eight libraries in Rome. Many of the books were by Greeks, but Rome did produce a few outstanding authors of its own. They mostly lived at the time of Augustus, who gave great help and encouragement to writers. Among them was Livy, who spent forty years writing his *History of Rome*, and many poets, including Horace and Virgil. Horace loved the countryside and often wrote about it. He also praised Augustus for bringing the civil wars to an end. But perhaps the greatest poet of all was Virgil. His most famous work, *Aeneid*, was written in honour of Augustus. It is a long story in verse about the Trojan hero Aeneas, who was supposed to have been an ancestor of Romulus and Remus.

Man with a scroll. The woman behind him stands for a lesser goddess called a *Muse*. She is helping him to write.

43 Religion and the Rise of Christianity

Like the Greeks, the early Romans believed there were spirit gods all around them—in the home, the earth, sea and sky, the rivers, forests and fields. These gods were thought to influence every human action, for good or evil. Therefore the people tried to please them. They built altars and temples and they offered sacrifices. Roman religion was a straightforward bargain. The people honoured their gods, who, in return, were supposed to bring good luck. No one ever loved a god or expected a god to love him. It came as a great surprise when, in the first century A.D., Christians began to preach about their God of love, mercy and forgiveness.

Roman gods

The gods of the household were called *Lares* and *Penates*. The first were supposed to protect the home and bring the family good fortune; the second made sure the store cupboard was never empty. There were also the *Manes*, the departed spirits of ancestors. Their happiness in the underworld was thought to depend on the respect given them by their living relations. On a shelf in the atrium there was usually a shrine or altar with little statues representing the household gods and the family's ancestors. Offerings of flowers, fruit and wine were made to them at the start of the day and before dinner in the evening.

The Romans also had gods which watched over the town and country as a whole. Under the influence of the Greeks, these became equal to the gods of Olympus (see Chapter 24). For example the Roman gods *Jupiter*, *Juno* and *Minerva*, whose temple was on the Capitol Hill, were the same as the Greek gods Zeus, Hera and Athena. Instead of Hestia, the Roman goddess of the hearth and home was called *Vesta*. At her temple, in the Forum, there burned an ever-

Remains of the temple of Vesta in the Roman forum

Sacrifice of a calf

lasting fire, looked after by priestesses called Vestal Virgins. Other Roman gods (Greek names in brackets) included *Neptune* (Poseidon) *Mars* (Ares) and *Mercury* (Hermes). The goddess of love and beauty was *Venus* (Aphrodite) and she had a little son called *Cupid*.

On festival days the chief priests made offerings to the gods. Animals were sacrificed and their livers were cut out. These were carefully inspected, for the priests claimed they could discover signs (omens) showing the will of the gods. Signs were also seen in things like thunder, lightning and the flight of birds. Like the Greeks, Romans were very superstitious. They would never attempt to do anything important if the omens were not favourable.

From the time of Augustus onwards the emperor himself became a god. In the provinces, sacred altars were set up and it was the duty of every citizen to join in worshipping the emperor's statue. By then large numbers of people had lost faith in the old gods. In Italy and the western provinces they began to turn to Eastern beliefs, which did more to comfort doubts and fears. Some promised an after-life, like the Egyptian gods Isis and Osiris, or Mithras, the Persian sun god. Soldiers were especially attracted to Mithras, for he was believed to give courage and eternal life.

Meanwhile, many educated people began to disbelieve *all* gods. They agreed with certain Greek thinkers who claimed there was no after-life and advised men to try to achieve happiness on earth. In the midst of all these different ideas, Christianity began to spread from the eastern Mediterranean.

Early Christians and the persecutions

Christ was born during the reign of Augustus, in Judaea, a province of Palestine. The date was not A.D. 1, as we might expect, but a little earlier; probably 4 B.C. Thus our present method of counting the years is not quite correct.

We can read about the life and teachings of Jesus in the New Testament. He was about thirty when he left Nazareth and began to travel through Palestine preaching to the people. Great crowds gathered to hear him; attracted by his religion of love and his promise of heaven for the faithful. They went away believing Jesus was the *Messiah* or Saviour, whose coming had been foretold by the prophets (see Chapter 20).

But the chief priests and other Jewish leaders refused to accept the word of Jesus. They expected a great and glorious Messiah, not a carpenter's son who favoured the poor and unfortunate. Jealous of his popularity, they warned Pontius Pilate, the governor, that Jesus was a danger to the peace and good order of Roman government. Although Pilate believed Jesus was innocent, he allowed the Jewish leaders to crucify him in A.D. 29.

The *disciples* (followers) of Jesus now took up the task of preaching the Christian message. The book of the Acts of the Apostles tells how Christianity was spread; first through Syria and then to Asia Minor, Greece and Rome itself. The conversion of the Gentiles (non-Jewish people) was led by St Paul, a successful businessman from Tarsus in Asia Minor. At first Paul was a strong opponent of Christianity, but one day, on the road to Damascus, he had a vision of Christ. From then on he devoted his life to preaching the new faith and organising groups of Christians into the first churches.

Christians made themselves unpopular with the Romans when they criticised slavery and the cruel sports of the amphitheatre. But the thing that really got them into trouble was their refusal to worship the emperor. Some were arrested and thrown into prison. The rest found themselves blamed for all kinds of disasters and misfortunes. When a great fire destroyed part of Rome in A.D. 64. Nero turned the anger of the people on the Christians. They were accused of starting the fire and hundreds of them were burnt at the stake in the emperor's

Victims sacrificed to wild animals. Some Christians were killed in this way

garden, like torches in the night.

This was the real start of the persecutions, which lasted for almost 250 years. Under some emperors thousands of Christians were crucified, burnt or thrown to the lions. At other times they were not killed just for their beliefs, although they were severely punished if they refused to worship the emperor's statue. Christians were forced to meet in secret and to hold their services in *catacombs* (underground caves). But this made people even more suspicious of them, for it was feared they were plotting against the government.

The acceptance of Christianity

Despite the persecutions the Christian Church went on growing. Its strongest support came from poor people, given new hope by Christ's promise of heaven for those who lived by his teachings. But the rich also took up the new faith. They admired Christians for the goodness of their lives, their care of the sick and the courage they showed in dying for their beliefs.

As Christianity spread throughout the Empire, regular councils were held to discuss doctrine (the teachings of the Church) and methods of organisation. In addition to ordinary priests, bishops were

In this sculpture Christ is shown as the Good Shepherd

appointed in all the main cities. We are told that the first bishop of Rome was St Peter, and that he was executed, along with St Paul, at the time of Nero. Later bishops of Rome were regarded as leaders of the Church. They got the name of Pope from the word *papa*, meaning father.

The last full scale persecution of Christians was carried out by Diocletian (284–305). But he was fighting a losing battle, for Christianity was by then the chief religion in the Empire. Realising this, the emperor Constantine ordered that all religions, including Christianity, should have complete freedom of worship (A.D. 313). He was eventually baptised a Christian on his deathbed (337).

The future of Christianity was assured. But there were still obstacles to overcome. In the backward country areas there were many non-believers. They were called pagans; from the Latin *paganus,* meaning a peasant or villager. In 361 the emperor Julian tried to revive the old pagan religions. But he was killed two years later, fighting the Persians. Pagan worship was finally forbidden in 392 by the emperor Theodosius. The old temples were closed and everyone in the Roman Empire was ordered to attend Christian services.

44 Decline and Fall

After two centuries of peace, prosperity and strong government, the Roman Empire began to weaken from about A.D. 200. One of the main causes of the decline was the repeated attacks of barbarian tribes along the Rhine and Danube frontiers. A line of strong emperors might have held back the invaders and kept the Empire safe and united. But this did not happen. The emperor Marcus Aurelius (161–180) gave up the idea of choosing an outstanding man to follow him. Instead he handed over power to his son Commodus, a boy of nineteen. It was a serious mistake. After twelve years full of plots and executions Commodus was strangled and civil war returned.

With no fixed method of choosing the next emperor there was nothing to stop cruel and selfish men from fighting for power. Time after time successful generals marched their legions to Rome and killed the reigning emperor, only to suffer the same fate themselves. In the space of seventy-three years (211–284) there were twenty-

The Roman Empire Divided, A.D. 395

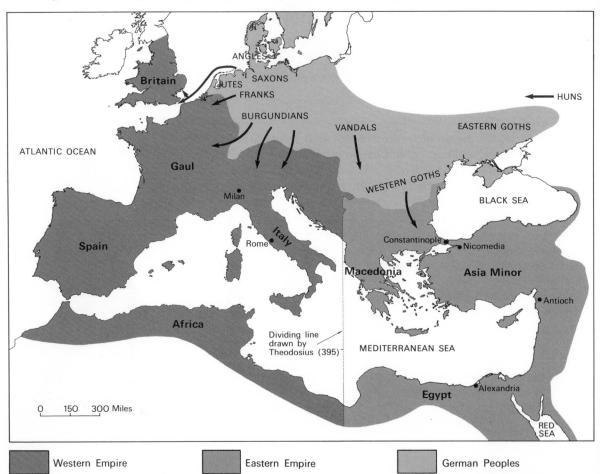

Western Empire   Eastern Empire   German Peoples

three emperors, and twenty of them were murdered. During this period the duties of government were often neglected. Robbers and pirates began to threaten trade routes by land and sea. There were serious famines in some of the provinces. To make matters worse, the population was falling, at a time when taxes had to be increased to pay for extra soldiers to defend the frontiers.

The division of the Empire

The decline was halted for a time by Diocletian (284–305). Large areas of farmland had been abandoned, resulting in food shortages. Diocletian put a stop to this by forbidding farmers and their sons from doing any other kind of work. The same rules were applied to certain essential trades.

Diocletian decided it was no longer possible for one man to govern the whole Empire. Therefore he ruled the East, from his palace at Nicomedia in Asia Minor, while a soldier called Maximian looked after the West. In 305 Diocletian retired, thinking his work was done. But immediately there was a series of struggles between rivals for the throne.

Order was restored by Constantine (307–37) who was proclaimed emperor by his soldiers at York in Britain. Realising Rome was too far away from the threatened frontiers, Constantine transferred the capital to Byzantium, which he renamed Constantinople (330). The West had its own governor, and later its own emperor. Although Constantine did not intend to split the Empire, from then on Italy and the western provinces were seriously weakened.

Diocletian's palace at Split in Yugoslavia, where he retired. This is the inner courtyard. People are still living in it, as you can see from the shutters on the windows

When Theodosius died (395) the Roman Empire finally broke into two separate pieces, each with its own emperor. The East, ruled from Constantinople, remained strong and well defended. It contained the most highly civilised countries, like Greece, Asia Minor, Syria and Egypt, with great trading cities like Alexandria and Antioch. But the Western Empire, centred on Rome or some other Italian city like Milan, grew steadily weaker. In less than 100 years it collapsed.

'Barbarian' on a monument in Rome

The barbarian invasions

We usually think of a barbarian as a brutal and uncivilised person. But in the days of the Roman Empire all foreigners living beyond the Rhine-Danube frontier were called barbarians, however civilised they may have been. These tall, fair-haired people were not as refined or educated as most Roman citizens, but they were far from being wild savages. Although they had no towns, they lived in villages, farmed the land and kept cattle and sheep. They belonged to many different tribes, such as the Goths, Vandals, Franks, Angles and Saxons. Together they were known as Germans, although many other races are descended from them, including the English, Dutch and Scandinavian peoples.

For centuries barbarian tribes had been trying to get inside the Roman frontiers. They wanted to settle further south, in a milder climate, and trade with the people of the provinces. But there was not enough land for everyone, so the legions drove them back each time they tried to invade the Empire. However, by the end of the second century the Romans were having increasing difficulty in defending all the frontiers. As the population fell, Rome was forced to come to terms with some of the German leaders. Their people were allowed to settle in underpopulated areas within the Empire and some of their warriors joined the Roman army.

But a dramatic change came towards the end of the fourth century, when a new and terrible enemy appeared. It was the fierce Huns, wandering herdsmen from central Asia, who were moving west to find fresh grasslands for their cattle and horses. They were dark-haired, short and stocky, with small slanting eyes and flat noses. Their unexpected arrival resulted in great stirrings among all the peoples of northern and central Europe.

In A.D. 376, about 100,000 Goths were allowed to cross the Danube frontier to shelter from the Huns. But before long thousands more were swarming into the Empire without permission. The Romans were powerless to stop them. Their policy of hiring barbarians to fight with the legions meant they had handed over some of the defence of the Empire to the people who were invading them! The Germans soon realised the Romans had no reserves behind the front line troops. Once the frontier was broken it could not be restored.

The Goths soon marched westwards, overrunning Greece and then Italy. In 410 their chieftain, Alaric, led them into Rome itself. For two days they ransacked the once mighty city—the first time it had

The Barbarian West
in the fifth century

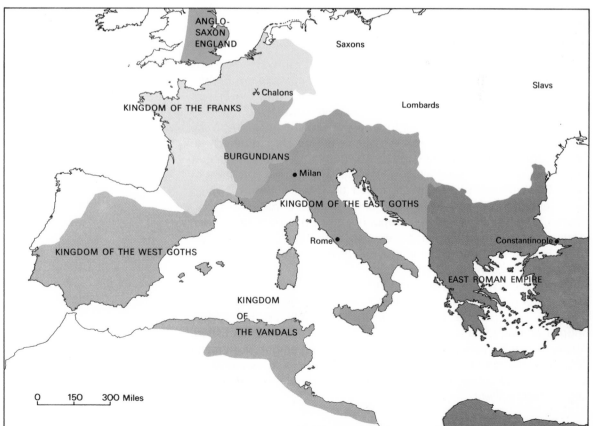

been captured since the invasion of the Gauls, 800 years before. In despair, the Romans recalled their legions from Britain.

Meanwhile, early in 406 the Rhine froze hard. Great hordes of Franks and Burgundians swarmed across the river and began to settle in Gaul. Further east, the Vandals burst into the Empire and soon overran Spain. Later, the western Goths settled in Spain and southern Gaul, while the Vandals conquered a large part of Roman North Africa. Gradually the whole Western Empire was divided into barbarian kingdoms. Even Britain, left undefended, was invaded across the North Sea by Angles, Saxons and Jutes.

By then the Huns had conquered eastern Europe. In 450 a great wave of them, under their dreaded leader Attila, poured across the Rhine into Gaul. The Goths joined with the remains of the Roman army to fight the common enemy, at Châlons. After a long and terrible battle the Huns were defeated (451). They eventually settled on the plains of Hungary.

In 455 Rome was ransacked again; this time by Vandals. For two whole weeks they plundered sacred buildings, including the emperor's palace on the Palatine Hill. Tons of valuables were taken down to the river and loaded on to their waiting ships. The Western Empire was now almost at an end. In 476 its last emperor, Romulus Augustulus, was removed by a Gothic leader, Odoacer, who proclaimed himself King of Italy.

The Roman Empire was not completely dead. The eastern part, later called Byzantium, resisted all invasions for another thousand years. But the emperors that ruled at Constantinople did not speak Latin and no longer had any connection with Rome.

Coin showing Romulus Augustulus, the last Western Emperor

What the Romans gave Europe

The German invaders spoiled many towns and allowed the roads to decay. But in other ways they were greatly affected by Roman civilisation. Some tribes had been in close contact with the Empire for centuries. They could appreciate its achievements.

Rome continued to be the headquarters of Christianity in the West. Many barbarians were already Christians before they entered the Empire. Roman law and language also lived on. The Romans taught millions of people to have respect for order and justice. The laws of many European nations today are based on those of Rome (which by the end of the Empire were much fairer and more reasonable than the old 'Twelve Tables' of early republican days). In the same way, modern languages like French, Spanish and Italian are based on Latin. English is closer to the languages of the German tribes, but it still has many Latin-based words.

The Romans were less artistic and less inventive than many other ancient peoples, notably the Greeks. But they were much more practical. They had the finest army, and they built the best roads, bridges and aqueducts. Under them trade and industry flourished. Above all, the Romans knew how to govern a vast empire, with many different races, religions and customs. As conquerors, these stubborn, disciplined and rather bloodthirsty men were more just than any people before them.

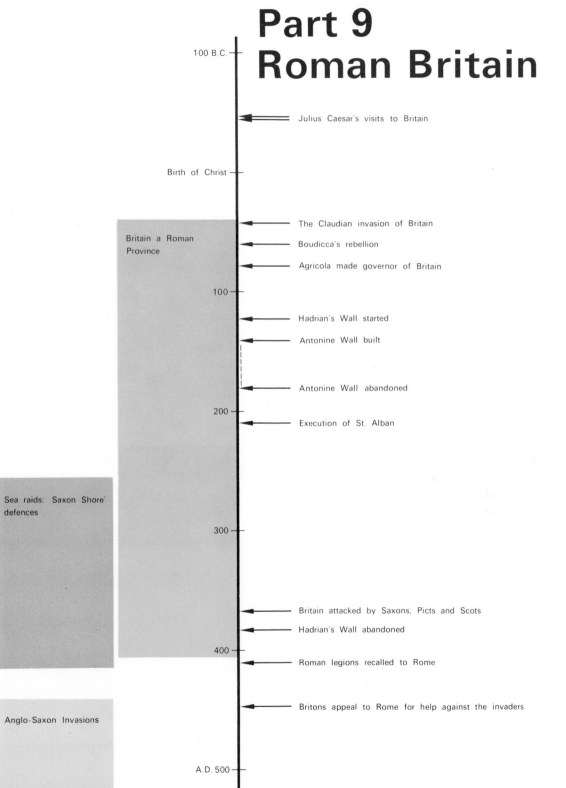

Part 9
Roman Britain

100 B.C.

Julius Caesar's visits to Britain

Birth of Christ

The Claudian invasion of Britain

Britain a Roman
Province

Boudicca's rebellion

Agricola made governor of Britain

100

Hadrian's Wall started

Antonine Wall built

Antonine Wall abandoned

200

Execution of St. Alban

Sea raids: Saxon Shore'
defences

300

Britain attacked by Saxons, Picts and Scots

Hadrian's Wall abandoned

400

Roman legions recalled to Rome

Britons appeal to Rome for help against the invaders

Anglo-Saxon Invasions

A.D. 500

45 A Visitor from Gaul

One morning in the summer of 55 B.C. a fleet of about eighty ships was seen approaching the coast of Britain, at the point where Dover now stands. Made of oak, with sails of leather or skins, these vessels came from Gaul, where they were commonly used for trading. But this time there were no merchants on board. The ships carried two legions of Roman soldiers; more than 10,000 of the world's best equipped and most highly trained fighting men. They were commanded by the great Julius Caesar, conqueror of Gaul.

The people of the Mediterranean lands had known about Britain for at least 500 years before Caesar's time. Carthaginian merchants visited its shores and carried away valuable cargoes of tin. But not until Caesar came was there any real connection between Britain and the Roman Empire. In the previous five years Caesar had advanced the frontier of the Empire as far north as the Channel. Now he set out to explore Britain. He claimed that its people had been helping the Gauls in their wars against Rome. But he had other reasons for visiting the country. He knew that he would gain even greater popularity in Rome if he could conquer this mysterious country, which Romans called 'the islands at the end of the earth'.

JVLIVS CÆSAR
MADE HIS FIRST LANDING IN BRITAIN
ON DEAL FORESHORE ON AVGVST 25TH 55 B·C
THIS TABLET WAS VNVEILED ON THE 25TH AVGVST 1946 BY
THE MAYOR OF DEAL, MR COVNCILLOR SIDNEY LITTLE J·P
TO COMMEMORATE THE 2000TH ANNIVERSARY OF THE LANDING

Memorial of Caesar's landing at Deal

Merchant ship like the ones Caesar used to cross the Channel

The first landing, 55 B.C.

Caesar wrote a full description of all his campaigns. Thus for the first time we have written records of an event in the country's history. Much of the account which follows is in Caesar's own words, translated from the original Latin.

'Even if there was not time for a campaign that season,' wrote Caesar, 'it would be of great advantage . . . merely to visit the island, to see what its inhabitants were like.' But the Britons were determined to stop the Romans from landing. News of Caesar's movements regularly came from Gaul, so the appearance of his fleet on the horizon caused no surprise. When he came close to the shore he could see 'the armed forces of the enemy posted on all the cliffs'. To avoid landing at a point where the Britons could hurl their weapons from a height, Caesar sailed up the coast for about seven miles. He finally 'ran his ships aground on an evenly sloping beach'—probably close to the spot where Deal now stands.

According to Caesar, 'the natives . . . had sent forward their cavalry and a number of chariots, which they regularly use in warfare; the rest of their forces followed close behind, and tried to prevent our troops from landing'. Some of the Britons stood on the shore, firing arrows and hurling javelins or stones. Others charged into the water. 'These perils frightened our soldiers,' wrote Caesar; 'inexperienced in this sort of fighting, our troops did not advance with the same fire and enthusiasm as they usually did in battles on dry land.'

Nevertheless, after fierce fighting the Britons were forced to give way before the better discipline of the Roman forces. They retreated and their leaders asked for peace. Unfortunately for Caesar he had only advanced a short distance inland when news reached him of storms and high tides on the coast. 'Several ships went to pieces,' he wrote, 'and others, having lost their cables, anchors and the rest of their tackle, were made useless for sailing.' Caesar quickly changed his plans. At his orders, 'timber and bronze from the most severely damaged vessels was used to repair the others'; with the result that 'all but twelve ships were saved and made fairly seaworthy.' Some days later, 'taking advantage of a spell of fair weather, he set sail . . . and the whole fleet reached the Continent safely'.

Who were the Britons?

The people whom Caesar had fought were closely related to the Gauls. Both the Britons and the Gauls were descended from the powerful Celtic race, which had settled in large areas of north-western Europe several hundred years before. Celts normally had fair or red hair and blue eyes. They were generally taller and more strongly built than the Mediterranean peoples. They were also less civilised, of course, although they were not the hairy savages they are often imagined to be.

Celts settled mostly in the south-east of England; on light soils like those of Salisbury Plain and the east coast. They built wooden farm houses, grew corn and reared cattle and sheep. For defence in tribal wars they built forts on the tops of hills, surrounded by huge banks and deep ditches. Remains of these hill-forts can still be seen

Julius Caesar

in some areas. The most famous is Maiden Camp in Dorset, which is more than half a mile long.

Maiden Camp

In the upland areas of the north and west the people were less advanced. But they must have learned many things from the Celts, including possibly their language. The Celts were the first people in Britain to use iron. It had the advantage of being much more plentiful than copper and tin, which the earlier Britons used for making bronze. Iron is harder than bronze, and therefore better for making tools and weapons. Iron bars of different sizes were at one time used as money, but coins of all kinds (some of them gold) were plentiful by the time of the Roman invasion. The Celts were the first people in Britain to ride horses and to use chariots. They also introduced the art of making pottery on a wheel.

Celtic bronze mirror: it would have been polished to show a good reflection

Only about twenty years before Caesar landed, a wave of new settlers came to Britain. They were the Belgae, a mixed race of Celts and Germans, who were attracted to lands around the mouth of the Thames, extending from present day Kent and Essex inland as far as Hertfordshire. The Belgae were more advanced than the Celts. They made many clearings in the forests and tried to farm the heavier soils with their metal-tipped plough.

Invasion, 54 B.C.

Caesar returned to Britain in the summer of 54 B.C. This time he was prepared for a full-scale invasion, with no less than five legions and 2,000 cavalry in several hundred ships. According to Caesar, the Britons, 'alarmed by the sight of so many ships . . . had retreated from the shore to hide themselves on higher ground'.

Once again the Roman fleet was anchored off an open beach, after which, we are told, 'a night march of about twelve miles brought

Caesar within sight of the enemy'. They . . . 'tried to bar his way by attacking from a position on higher ground', but the disciplined Romans proved too strong for them. The Britons were forced to retreat, after suffering heavy losses. Before Caesar could press home his advantage he heard that a sudden storm had again damaged most of his ships. Ten precious days were lost while the whole fleet was drawn up on the beach and made seaworthy once more. About forty ships were beyond repair.

When Caesar again marched inland 'larger British forces had now been assembled from all sides, and by common consent they had given the overall command and conduct of the campaign to Cassivellaunus'. He was the leader of the Catuvellauni, the most powerful tribe of Belgae. After several days of hard fighting, however, Caesar was able to cross the Thames. Cassivellaunus, realising the Romans could not be defeated in open battle, withdrew about 4,000 charioteers and tried to upset the invading army with surprise attacks from hidden positions. When this failed he retired to a stronghold among the woods; possibly at Wheathampstead in Hertfordshire. It was surrounded by marshes and protected by an earth wall and ditch.

The Romans immediately stormed the stronghold. Caesar tells us that 'after a short time the enemy proved unable to resist the violent attack of the legions, and rushed out of the fortress on another side . . . many of those trying to escape were captured or killed'. Cassivellaunus sent a message of surrender and promised to pay money and goods to Rome. But Caesar had already decided to abandon the invasion, ' for fear any sudden rising should break out in Gaul'. He led his army back to the coast and returned to the Continent.

It is difficult to say whether Caesar hoped to conquer Britain in 54 B.C., or whether he intended to return at a later date. As it happened, events in Gaul kept him fully occupied for the next few years, after which he marched in triumph to Rome (49 B.C.).

The ditch at
Wheathampstead

After Caesar's invasion, nearly a hundred years went by before a Roman army was again seen in Britain. Civil wars in Rome put a stop to all foreign adventures for some time. Then, when these were over, Augustus spent more than forty years restoring peace and order. He believed the Empire had reached its natural limits and had no wish to begin further costly campaigns overseas.

But many Romans believed that the Gauls would always be restless and troublesome as long as Britain was left unconquered. Rebels from Gaul sometimes escaped across the Channel to Britain, and it was feared that they were plotting against Roman rule. When the emperor Claudius (A.D. 41–54) came to power an invasion of Britain was at last planned. There were troops to spare, for the Rhine and Danube frontiers were peaceful, and Claudius was eager to begin his reign in a blaze of glory. It was thought that the cost of the campaign would be more than repaid by the extra taxes and increased trade that would result. Britain was known to be rich in metals, including silver and tin, and it was a good land for growing wheat and raising cattle.

Bronze head of the Emperor Claudius

The Claudian invasion

In A.D. 43 Claudius sent an invasion force of 40,000 men, commanded by Aulus Plautius, an experienced general. It was much stronger in cavalry than Caesar's army had been, and was thus better suited to British warfare. In other ways the Romans had learned from Caesar's experiences. Instead of landing on an open beach, Plautius sailed a few miles up the coast and found a sheltered harbour at Richborough. Here ships could ride safely at anchor.

As expected, the Britons put up a hard fight; especially the Catuvellauni tribe, which now controlled most of the south-east. After several minor battles a decisive contest was fought beside the river Medway. The brave Britons had little chance against the disciplined Roman army, yet the invaders took nearly two days to break through. The leader of the Catuvellauni, Caratacus, lived to fight another day. Realising the hilly regions of the west might be more difficult to conquer, he fled to Wales. There he gathered a group of supporters and prepared to resist the Roman advance.

After crossing the Thames, Plautius called a halt and sent for Claudius to come and receive in person the surrender of several British tribal chiefs. This took place at Colchester, which had become an important centre of the Catuvellauni. It was not really a town; just a collection of scattered huts, surrounded by earth banks for defence. Claudius only stayed a fortnight in Britain. Before returning to Rome to celebrate victory he made Plautius the governor and left him instructions for the conquest of the rest of the country.

The Roman Conquest of Britain

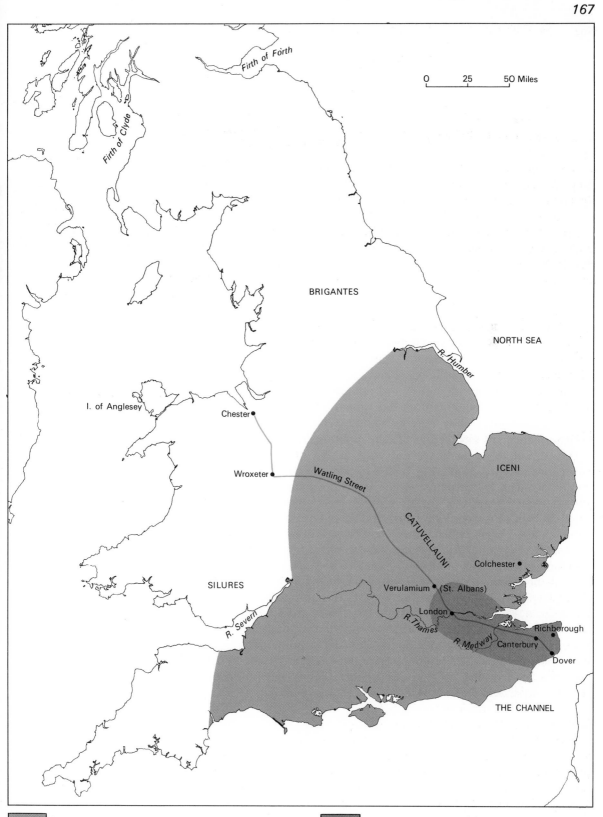

Firth of Forth

Firth of Clyde

BRIGANTES

NORTH SEA

R. Humber

I. of Anglesey

Chester

ICENI

Wroxeter

Watling Street

CATUVELLAUNI

Colchester

SILURES

Verulamium (St. Albans)

London

R. Severn

R. Thames

Richborough

R. Medway

Canterbury

Dover

THE CHANNEL

0   25   50 Miles

Area conquered by Aulus Plautius (43-47 A.D.)   Area invaded by Caesar (54 B.C.)

The tribes that had been defeated were the most advanced in Britain. But if Plautius expected less resistance from those further inland he was soon disappointed. Some tribes held out in their hill-forts and the Romans suffered heavy casualties storming them. At Maiden Camp (captured in A.D. 44) archaeologists have unearthed large numbers of skeletons from this period which show the marks of a bitter struggle. Many were beheaded or had smashed skulls.

After more than three years of hard fighting, Roman armies had occupied Britain as far north and west as the rivers Humber and Severn. As they advanced they built a network of roads. The Britons only had tracks or footpaths, which were unsuitable for marching large numbers of soldiers. Therefore the Roman legions had to spend much of their time quarrying stone and building roads and bridges. Extra labourers were obtained from conquered tribes.

Most of the main roads in Roman Britain were built soon after the invaders arrived. They followed direct routes, sometimes cutting through belts of uninhabited forest. One of the first was Watling Street, which ran from the Kent coast, through Canterbury and London, to Wroxeter and Chester. The route from London was roughly the same as that followed today by the A5 road. Altogether 5000 miles of roads were built by the Romans in Britain. The best of them were as good as those in the Mediterranean provinces. They had firm foundations of stone and rubble, a smooth surface of paving stones, and drainage ditches.

Caratacus and Boudicca

The Romans soon discovered that Britain was divided roughly into two natural regions. The first, a lowland area extending from the south-east coast to the Midlands, had already been occupied by A.D. 47. The second region, the north and west, which contained many upland areas, proved more difficult to conquer—even though it was thinly populated.

Bolt from a Roman catapult embedded in the spine of a Briton found at Maiden Camp. It had entered the body from the front

When the Romans advanced into the hills of South Wales they met fierce resistance from a tribe called the Silures. These were organised and led by Caratacus, who had escaped after the battle of the Medway. He knew it would be suicide to meet the Roman army face to face in open battle. Instead he divided his men into small groups, scattered among the hills. From well concealed hideouts they made surprise raids on the Romans, retreating before the enemy had a chance to recover.

After nearly two years of fighting Caratacus was finally defeated, in North Wales (A.D. 51). He escaped for a time, but Cartimandua, queen of a northern tribe called the Brigantes, handed him over to the Romans after falsely promising to help him. Caratacus was put in chains and sent to Rome. But Claudius was so impressed by his spirit and courage that he pardoned him and allowed him to live freely in the capital. The next few years were fairly peaceful. In the Roman occupied areas of Britain roadbuilding continued, the first towns were established and forts were built as bases for the legions (see Chapter 48).

The Roman advance into Wales was successfully continued in A.D. 59, when an experienced soldier, Suetonius Paulinus, became Governor. Marching through the mountains, he had reached the Isle of Anglesey when news came of a serious uprising led by the Iceni, a tribe from what is now Norfolk. Their queen, Boudicca (often called Boadicea) had been very roughly treated by some Roman troops. In fury, the Iceni took up arms and were supported by neighbouring tribesmen.

In A.D. 60 Boudicca's forces attacked the Roman town of Colchester and burned it to the ground. Its citizens were slaughtered. The nearest legion was more than 100 miles away, so Boudicca, riding at the head of her army in a chariot, made for London—the site of another Roman town. Within a few days both London and nearby Verulamium (St Albans) had been reduced to ashes.

This layer of ash found below London was probably caused by Boudicca's attack

Site of a legionary camp in Scotland

Suetonius's main army now arrived from Wales, having marched along Watling Street. They were outnumbered ten to one, but their superior weapons and discipline again proved the deciding factor. Boudicca foolishly allowed her forces to advance between two areas of woodland, where they crowded together so closely that they got in each other's way. Choosing the right moment to charge, the Romans cut them to pieces. Boudicca poisoned herself to avoid capture, but thousands of her supporters were rounded up and massacred.

A great governor

In the next six years the Romans regained firm control of the southeast. The three ruined towns were rebuilt and peace was restored. Not until the years A.D. 71–78 did Roman armies again advance into the upland areas. The most troublesome tribes—the Brigantes and the Silures—were defeated and great fortresses for the legions were built at York, Caerleon and Chester.

In A.D. 78 Gnaeus Julius Agricola was made governor. He already had wide experience of Britain, having served in the country first as a

Remains of a permanent
stone fort at Housesteads
on Hadrian's Wall

young officer and then, some years later, as commander of a legion.
In the next five years Agricola almost completed the Roman conquest
of Britain. After crushing all remaining opposition in Wales and
northern England, he marched into Caledonia (Scotland) building
forts and roads on the way. He reached the rivers Clyde and Forth
without serious opposition, but he wisely decided not to attempt a
difficult and dangerous campaign in the Highlands. Agricola con-
tented himself with a crushing victory over some Highland tribes at
the battle of Mons Graupius (A.D. 83).

By the time Agricola was recalled to Rome (84) he had occupied all
the mainland of Britain up to central Scotland. But he was more than
a general on the battlefield. He took a keen interest in the British people,
helping them to educate themselves and encouraging them to take up
Roman customs. We know a lot about the governorship of Agricola
because his daughter was married to a writer called Tacitus, who
wrote a great deal about his father-in-law. 'Agricola,' said Tacitus,
'made the people realise that under good laws it was better to live at
peace with the Romans, rather than to rebel against them.'

47 Building a Frontier

As the Highland tribes recovered from the defeat of Mons Graupius they began to attack the northernmost forts built by Agricola. The Romans, greatly outnumbered, were forced to abandon the forts, one by one. In about A.D. 117 the tribes from Scotland made a full-scale raid into northern England, causing widespread destruction. It was clear that the emperor, Hadrian (117–38), would have to do something to stop these disturbances.

Hadrian's Wall

In 122 Hadrian travelled to Britain. He was the first reigning emperor to visit the province since Claudius, nearly eighty years before. Like Agricola, Hadrian realised the Highlands could not be conquered without a huge army and enormous trouble and expense. He also saw that most of Britain was peaceful and prosperous under Roman rule.

The Emperor Hadrian

Roman soldiers often enjoyed the comforts of town living: Chesters fort on the Wall had its own bath house

A stretch of Hadrian's Wall near Housesteads fort

The emperor therefore decided to cut the country in two with a permanent walled frontier, running from coast to coast. Such a wall would, as he put it, 'separate the Romans and the barbarians'.

Hadrian chose to make the frontier at a point where the British mainland is only seventy-three miles across. It ran from Bowness-on-Solway in the west to Wallsend-on-Tyne in the east, defending an area roughly equal to present day England and Wales. It was the task of the legions to construct the great wall, although many local Britons were forced to help them. First of all foundations were laid in trenches. Then the outsides of the wall, eight to ten feet apart, were built from carefully trimmed stones and the space between them was packed with a mixture of broken stones and mortar. Turf was used in some places, where stone was difficult to get. When completed, the wall was twenty feet high, including battlements and a sentry walk along the top.

About 14,000 soldiers were needed to patrol and defend the frontier—a third of the total Roman army in Britain. These were housed in forts, castles and turrets, which were built at regular intervals along the whole length of the wall.

Spaced out roughly five miles apart were sixteen large forts. They were built on to the main frontier and had similar high stone walls on their other three sides. Roads entered these forts through well guarded gateways in the centre of each wall. Inside there were barracks large enough to hold a cohort of soldiers (500 or more) as well as stables, a hospital, workshops for stonemasons, carpenters and blacksmiths, and granaries (grain stores) with raised floors to prevent the corn from getting damp.

Filling the gaps between the forts were *milecastles*, so called because they were roughly a mile apart. (But remember a Roman mile was only about 1,620 yards.) There were eighty of these castles along the whole length of the wall, each holding up to 100 men. Between pairs of milecastles were two watchtowers or *turrets*, about 540 yards apart. These were much smaller and contained sentries who took turns to keep watch. Soldiers in both the milecastles and the turrets were ready to pass on smoke signals (or light fires if it was dark) at the first sign of an attack. As well as keeping watch they acted as customs officers, inspecting all goods carried by traders crossing the wall.

As an extra defence against attack a V-shaped ditch, roughly nine feet deep, was dug along the north side of the wall, about twenty feet in front of it. On the south side the boundary of the military zone was marked by a trench called the *vallum*. Its main purpose was probably to prevent intruders and stray animals from coming too close to the wall and the adjoining buildings.

The construction of Hadrian's Wall can hardly have been finished before A.D. 127. Then roughly four more years would have been necessary for the completion of all the earthworks and buildings— including an extra system of forts and signal towers extending for forty miles down the west coast. For the next 250 years Hadrian's Wall protected the Roman province against the attacks of the barbarian tribes of the north. On the rare occasions when invaders got through they found it almost impossible to return with stolen cattle or crops. Indeed, they ran the risk of being trapped behind the wall, at the mercy of the Roman armies.

The Antonine Wall

After the death of Hadrian (138) Roman armies advanced north of the frontier and re-occupied many of the forts that had been built by Agricola in Scotland. By about 140 they began to construct a second frontier across the narrow neck of land between the estuaries of the Forth and the Clyde. It was a thirty-seven mile wall of turf; known as the Antonine Wall, after the emperor Antoninus Pius (138–61). It was much cheaper and simpler to build than Hadrian's Wall, for it had no milecastles or turrets and no vallum. Altogether its forts contained only six or seven thousand soldiers.

The Emperor Septimus Severus

The new frontier seems to have lasted for only about forty years. Around A.D. 180 tribes from central Scotland swept across the Antonine Wall and it was abandoned. The Romans retreated to Hadrian's Wall, which was the only frontier from now on.

After the emperor Commodus died (193) civil war broke out between rival claimants for the throne. One of them was Clodius Albinus, Governor of Britain, who took the legions away from the frontier to fight for him in Gaul (196–7). The Scottish tribes saw their chance. Immediately a wave of destruction swept over northern Britain. In some places Hadrian's Wall was completely demolished and the fortress at York was overrun.

Order was restored by the emperor Septimus Severus (193–211) who defeated Clodius and sent a new governor to Britain. The wall began to be rebuilt, and Severus later visited Britain to supervise its completion (208). The repairs were so extensive that for a long time historians believed that Severus actually built the wall. By the time he died, at York (211), the barbarian tribes had been defeated and pushed back into the Highlands. The British frontier now had almost a hundred years of peace.

48 Britain's First Towns

At the time of the Roman invasion the nearest thing to a town in Britain was a collection of huts protected by banks and ditches. But the Romans quickly set about building towns, which were essential to their way of life. It was through towns that they had spread their influence in other western provinces, like Spain and Gaul.

The modern names of many British towns are a guide to the position of former Roman settlements. For example, the Latin word for a camp or fort is *castra*, and we find many towns today whose names end in -chester, -caster or -cester. Manchester, Doncaster, Gloucester and dozens more were once Roman military settlements.

Tribal centres, 'colonies' and fortresses

The Romans turned former Celtic strongholds into market towns and centres of government for each tribal area. In this way towns like Cirencester, Canterbury, Verulamium, Silchester, Leicester and many others came into being. Where there had been hill-forts a new settlement was usually established on lower ground. For instance Maiden Camp was replaced by nearby Dorchester. But as far as possible the Romans aimed to develop existing settlements, no matter how small they were. Surveyors and architects were sent to plan the layout of streets and buildings, and the local people did most of the construction under their guidance.

Tribal leaders and other important Britons were usually made Roman citizens and encouraged to take up Roman customs, like the wearing of togas. They were also expected to play a part in local government. Each tribal centre had magistrates, elected every year by the people, and a town council, which was like a miniature Roman Senate. As well as keeping law and order, magistrates were expected to provide regular games and other entertainments.

In a few selected areas the Romans established a special kind of town called a *colonia*. This was a settlement or 'colony' of retired soldiers from the legions. Each received a plot of farming land in the surrounding countryside. The first colonia, at Colchester, was built soon after the Claudian invasion. It was still under construction in A.D. 60 when it was destroyed in Boudicca's rebellion; but it was soon rebuilt. Later on further 'colonies' were established at Lincoln, Gloucester and the military centre of York, which grew in importance after the building of Hadrian's Wall (see page 178).

London may also have been a colonia in later years, although we do not know for sure. In many ways London was different from all the other towns of Roman Britain. It was the centre of trade and business and the chief port of the province. Roads led to London from all directions, like the spokes of a wheel. A wooden bridge was built over the Thames, and by the second century London had become

Tombstone of a Roman surveyor, showing the instrument he used for measuring right-angles

one of the largest towns north of Italy.

Most of the country's exports were shipped from London; particularly iron and other metals, cattle, hides, hunting dogs and wheat. In return came many of the luxuries of the Roman world, such as glass tableware, fine pottery, silk, spices and wines. Before long London must have replaced Colchester as the main centre of government. It was almost certainly the financial headquarters and the place where coins were minted. The governor was probably stationed in or near London, as well as his deputy and his chief legal adviser.

Practically all the major towns were situated in the peaceful south-eastern part of Britain. Here the Roman way of life took firm root. But in the more troubled regions of the north and west the main settlements were forts. Three in particular—the great 'legionary

Modern painting of Roman
London as it probably
looked at the end of the
second century A.D.

A Roman cart

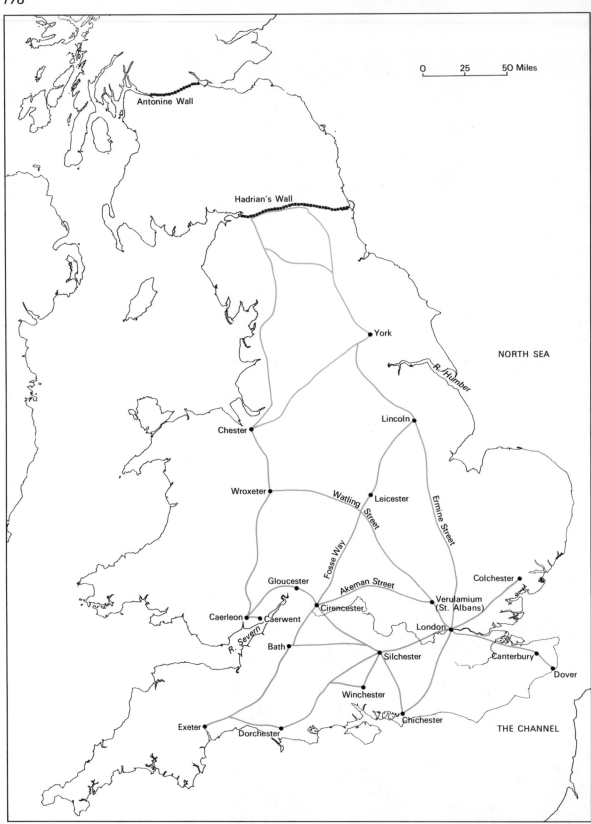

Antonine Wall

Hadrian's Wall

York

NORTH SEA

R. Humber

Lincoln

Chester

Wroxeter

Watling Street

Leicester

Ermine Street

Fosse Way

Gloucester

Akeman Street

Colchester

Cirencester

Verulamium
(St. Albans)

Caerleon

Caerwent

London

R. Severn

Bath

Silchester

Canterbury

Dover

Winchester

Chichester

THE CHANNEL

Exeter

Dorchester

0   25   50 Miles

The theatre at St. Albans: the stage was just in front of the pillar

fortresses' at York, Caerleon and Chester—were larger than many towns, with several thousand soldiers in each. At first their defences were made of wood and banks of earth, but these were soon replaced by huge stone walls and deep ditches. Inside were streets and public buildings, just like those in an ordinary town. On a much smaller scale, more than a hundred permanent forts were built in Britain, mostly on or near the northern frontier. Villages often grew up next to forts, to supply the soldiers with food and other essentials.

Town life

Generally speaking, the towns of Roman Britain were much smaller than those in the Mediterranean lands. Most of them had well under 5,000 inhabitants. It seems that expected increases in population never came, because the stone walls round many towns enclosed large areas of land that was never built on. But in other ways Britain's first towns were typically Roman. Each had a forum (market place) in or near the centre and a *basilica* (town hall) where public meetings and the law courts were held. There were also temples for religious worship and a public baths, which might be large enough to hold the entire population at the same time.

Amphitheatres were situated outside most of the main towns. Ordinary theatres might be built instead, as, for example, at Verulamium (St Albans) where both 'games' and theatrical performances

Main roads and towns in Roman Britain

were held. It is unlikely that British town dwellers saw entertainments as costly as those that thrilled the crowds in Rome (see Chapter 39). Instead of expensive animals like lions and leopards, they probably had bull- and bear-baiting, cockfighting and fights between gladiators. Chariot races must have been rare, although we know for sure that they were regularly held at Lincoln.

The houses in British towns were usually smaller and less comfortable than those in the Mediterranean provinces. Nevertheless wealthy families frequently had ten, twelve or more rooms, joined together by an outside corridor or verandah. They had special quarters for the household slaves and a separate kitchen and dining room. There were even flush lavatories and baths in the most luxurious houses. Some of the rooms, if not all of them, had a *hypocaust* system of under-floor heating, fed by a charcoal-fired furnace (see Chapter 41). This was more essential in Britain than in the warm climate of the Mediterranean lands, where it originated. Needless to say, these houses were decorated in Roman styles, with painted wall plaster and mosaic floors.

Wealthy Britons copied the Romans not only in the design of their houses but also in their dress, language and other customs. Schools were set up, similar to those in Rome (see Chapter 42), and educated slaves were employed as tutors to the younger children. If they had been made citizens of Rome (remember this was a special privilege before A.D. 213, when every freeborn subject in the Empire was granted citizenship) Britons proudly wore togas. They also spoke Latin. Before the Claudian invasion some British princes had begun to inscribe their coins with Latin words. After the conquest, Latin became the main language in the towns, where Celtic was probably used little, if at all. Even craftsmen and labourers could read and write Latin. We know this because words and remarks have been found scratched on tiles, bricks and pieces of pottery.

Workmen and shopkeepers, who made up a large proportion of every town population, lived in simple wooden houses with home-made furniture. These houses were often long and narrow, with one short side facing the street. The living quarters were at the back— the normal Roman practice, to shut out the noise of the streets. The front was usually a shop. The goods on sale might be expensive articles imported from the Continent. But more often they were local British products, like ironmongery, pottery and window glass, made in a workroom behind the shop. Every household, rich or poor, spun and wove most of its own cloth. In the later years of the Roman occupation British textiles were sold in large quantities all over the Empire.

Towards the end of the fourth century the towns in Roman Britain began to decline. They depended upon trade, yet the growing menace of the barbarian tribes endangered trade routes by land and sea in all the northern provinces of the Empire. As trade grew less British towns began to shrink in size. Some were kept alive only by the need to hold regular tribal councils and law courts. Many rich families moved to villas in the countryside. Tradesmen often went too, finding they could work just as well on a country estate as in a town.

49 The Countryside

In Britain and many other parts of Europe the building of towns was like a trademark of Roman occupation. But the overall importance of these settlements should not be exaggerated, for the daily lives of most Britons were hardly affected by them. Throughout the period of Roman rule a large majority of the population lived in the countryside and farmed the land in much the same way as their ancestors had done centuries before.

In some parts of the country the Celtic field pattern can still be seen from the air. This picture was taken in Dorset

Native farms

Most of Britain was still covered by dense woodland, but where clearings had been made peasant families lived, in their simple timber-framed huts or farmsteads. These were usually one-roomed and circular in shape. Nearby were pits, lined with clay or wicker-work, where dried grain was stored. It was usual for each family to make its own pottery and woollen cloth. In some areas peasants also made their owh tools and farming implements out of iron.

In the fertile lowlands of Britain the main crop was wheat, grown in small, square fields. Many peasants also kept pigs and either small flocks of sheep or herds of cattle. The wheelless plough of the Celts was only suitable for light soils, but the Belgae brought a heavier wheeled plough which was used to prepare the richer soils of the valleys. At harvest time the crops were cut with scythes or sickles. The Romans probably introduced an improved two-handed scythe and a spade with an iron blade. But otherwise they seem to have made little attempt to teach the Britons new farming methods.

In the upland areas most families kept cattle and sheep. Fields had to be fenced to protect the animals from wolves, which were then common in Britain. Probably many of the livestock had to be killed off as winter approached, because it must have been difficult to produce enough fodder to keep them all alive until the spring. The meat could be preserved with salt, to provide the family with food for the winter.

Many peasants, especially those living in remote hilly areas, hardly ever saw a Roman. The only real change in their lives resulting from the conquest was the Roman government's demand for taxes. At regular intervals they had to travel to a special collection point and hand over a certain amount of their produce—usually grain or hides. Some of it was sent to Rome, but a large proportion was kept to supply the army in Britain.

Villas

It is unlikely that the peasants owned the land they farmed. They had probably been granted it by the tribal chiefs, who received some of their produce in return. These powerful Britons also kept large estates for themselves, and it was here that the influence of the Romans could be seen most clearly. Celtic farm houses of wood, reeds and clay were rebuilt in the style of Roman villas, with solid stone foundations and walls of flint and mortar.

Depending on the wealth of its owner, a villa could be anything from a simple farm cottage to a great mansion with dozens of rooms and a large staff of servants and labourers. In Britain they were not holiday houses or 'pleasure villas', like those found in parts of Italy (see Chapter 41). They were centres of profit-making estates, owned by farmers rather than rich town dwellers. Most of them gradually grew in size and comfort throughout the period of Roman occupation. As well as the main living quarters, barns and other outbuildings were put up to house farm labourers and livestock and to store tools and the produce of the land. The villa itself might be built round a court-yard. If the owner was rich it would have a central heating system,

Corn measure—used for judging the amount of grain collected from native farmers

private baths, mosaic floors and decorated walls.

Larger villas often had their own workshops for blacksmiths, carpenters, weavers and other tradesmen. These supplied the essential needs of the estate. Villa owners might only visit a town when they wanted non-essential things like wine, olive oil, glass and luxury articles imported from other parts of the Empire. These were paid for by selling food, wool or hides produced on the estate.

Fine mosaic found in a large villa at Fishbourne, in Sussex

Hundreds of villas have been excavated in Britain. Roughly ninety per cent of them have been found in the south-eastern part of the country, below an imaginary line drawn from the Humber to the Bristol Channel. This area contained most of the good farming land and a majority of the population of Britain. But it is also likely that open settlements in northern and western regions were considered unsafe because of frequent raids by tribes beyond the frontiers.

Mining

Not all country dwellers farmed the land. Some of them worked in mines and stone quarries, which were scattered all over Britain. One of the reasons for the Roman conquest was their desire to profit from Britain's rich deposits of minerals. Most important were lead mines, which the Romans worked not only for the lead itself but for the silver which could be extracted from it. Within six years of the Claudian invasion, lead from the Mendip Hills (in Somerset) was already being exported to Gaul and Italy.

In earlier times the most famed of British metals was tin, mined in Cornwall. In fact, among ancient traders like the Phoenicians Britain was known as 'the Tin Isles'. But the output from the Cornish mines fell when larger deposits of tin were found in Spain, just before the Romans came to Britain. Not until the third century did the mines of Cornwall begin to recover some of their earlier importance.

Iron was mined in large quantities, particularly in the Sussex Weald, the Forest of Dean (near Gloucester) and other wooded areas, where plenty of charcoal could be produced for smelting the iron-ore. Copper, which was used for making bronze, was mostly obtained in North Wales. Coal was dug up in many areas and used as an ordinary domestic fuel. At least one Roman gold mine has been discovered, in South Wales.

Practically all the mines in Britain were taken over by the Roman government. The work was done by Britons, many of them slaves, prisoners or criminals. Transport often presented more difficulties than the actual mining. Even if there was a good road that could be used it was better to carry heavy goods like minerals on rivers or along the coast.

This lead bar is stamped with the Emperor Vespasian's name

50 Religious Beliefs

Like most pagan peoples, the ancient Britons worshipped a great variety of nature gods. The sea, sky, mountains, rivers and trees were believed to have powerful spirits, who demanded regular sacrifice and prayer. In some Celtic religions pigs, bulls, horses and snakes were also thought to have magical powers. Above all, Britons worshipped the sun (the source of light and warmth) and the moon (the measure of time).

The destruction of the Druids

The Romans usually allowed conquered peoples to keep their own religions. In Britain they did the same—with one important exception. The Celts had powerful priests called Druids, whose activities were strictly forbidden by the Romans. There were two main reasons for this. First, Druids acted as tribal judges, deciding disputes according to their own mysterious laws. Second, they carried out human sacrifices, from which they believed they could foretell the future.

Druids held religious services in special oak groves, which they considered to be sacred. First they cut some mistletoe. For this a golden knife was used, because mistletoe was believed to be holy when growing on an oak tree. The sprigs were gathered in a white sheet and distributed among the fathers of all the families present. Next came the sacrifices. In times of peace bulls were slaughtered, but in wartime human sacrifices were made. If no prisoners or criminals were available, an old man would be taken from the crowd. When his throat had been slit with a sacred knife, the Druids foretold the future by inspecting the flow of blood and the twitching of the victim's arms and legs.

A Celtic god, Taranus, which the Romans took over from the British

The Romans ordered that these brutal ceremonies must stop. They also insisted that Britain would be governed by their laws, not those of the Druids. When these commands were disobeyed the governor, Suetonius Paulinus, decided to wipe out the Druids by attacking their great stronghold on the Isle of Anglesey (A.D. 60). As the Roman soldiers came ashore, wild priestesses ran about holding flaming torches and the terrified priests screamed dreadful curses at the invaders. But Suetonius showed no mercy. The Druids were massacred and their sacred oak groves were chopped down. At this stage a messenger arrived bringing news of Boudicca's rebellion in East Anglia. Suetonius immediately returned to the mainland and began the long march eastwards. The rebellion had come just too late to save the Druids. Nothing more was heard of them in Britain.

Roman gods

The worship of gods like Jupiter, Juno and Minerva was going out of fashion by the time the Romans came to Britain (see Chapter 43).

Model showing what the temple of Claudius at Colchester probably looked like

The god Mithras

But emperor worship had now become an 'official' religion throughout the Empire.

Immediately after the invasion of A.D. 43, work started on a great temple to Claudius at Colchester. Stone was brought from far and wide, and no expense was spared in making it, because Colchester had been chosen as the centre of emperor worship for the whole province. Yearly gatherings of tribal leaders were held there. On these occasions promises of loyalty and prayers for the emperor's safety were offered. Public worship of the emperor was also carried out in the military settlements and in each colonia. Family altars were set up in a few homes. But on the whole the ordinary people of Britain showed little interest in emperor worship. They preferred their own gods.

Soldiers and merchants brought with them many different religions from Persia, Egypt, Syria, North Africa, Germany and many other parts of the Empire. The most highly organised was the worship of Mithras, a Persian god (see Chapter 43). Services were restricted to men only and held secretly in small temples with room for about a dozen worshippers at a time. Traces of these temples have been found mainly in the military areas of the north, including the forts along Hadrian's Wall.

Many wealthy British families began to worship Roman gods; especially if they had been made citizens of Rome. But they often found it hard to give up their old Celtic beliefs and customs. In most towns these continued alongside Roman forms of worship, and sometimes the two got mixed together.

Early Christianity

Little is known about the coming of Christianity to Britain. The faith was probably introduced during the second century, but it was slow in taking root. We are told that the first Briton to be put to death for being a Christian was Albanus (usually known as Alban), a citizen of Verulamium. He owned a house in the town where he sheltered a priest, to protect him from persecution. Albanus himself became a Christian, but he was soon found out and executed on top of a nearby hill, probably in the year 209. In later times a church was built there, and this is the spot where St Albans abbey now stands.

Christianity made slow progress in Britain until the early fourth century. Then, under the protection of the emperor Constantine (307–37), it came out into the open. In 314 the British Church was sufficiently organised to be able to send three bishops to the Council of Arles, in southern Gaul. British representatives attended three more general councils of the Church in the next thirty-five years.

Even so, it is likely that the number of Christians in the province was small and that most of them were poor. Because of this very few traces of Christian worship have been found among Roman remains in Britain. Part of what may have been a church has been dug up at Silchester. But otherwise the only findings of importance have been Christian wall paintings and mosaics in one or two villas. When the Romans left Britain (about 410) pagan beliefs must have been still very strong—even though Christianity was the official religion of the Empire after 392.

Roman mosaic showing Christian symbols. The Greek letters *khi* and *rho* (see p. 95) are the first two letters of the Greek word for Christ

Towards the end of the third century Britain began to be threatened by sea raids from Saxons, Franks and other barbarian peoples of northern Europe. Many of the raiders started out as pirates, attacking shipping in the Channel and the North Sea. Then they began to land along the east coast of Britain and carry away crops, livestock and anything else of value they could lay hands on. These raids continued until the fifth century, when a full-scale invasion took place. By then the Romans had gone and the way was open for hundreds of thousands of Angles, Saxons and Jutes to cross the seas and settle in Britain. The story of the Anglo-Saxon invasions is told in the second book in this series: *The Middle Ages.*

The 'Saxon Shore'

To protect the province against sea raids the Romans built a system of coastal defences along the 'Saxon Shore'. All round the southeast of Britain, from the Norfolk coast to the Isle of Wight, special forts were constructed, together with signal stations. These forts contained both soldiers and sailors, so they were able to deal with the raiders on land and sea. They could also be used as bases for sea patrols—carried out by small, fast craft which reported the move-

Roman fort on the 'Saxon Shore' at Portchester, in Hampshire. A Norman castle has been built in one corner, and a Saxon church in the other

ments of enemy ships to the Roman fleet.

These shore defences were fairly successful until the year 367, when Roman Britain was attacked by enemies on every side. Just as large numbers of Saxons were landing in the south-east, the northern frontier was attacked by land and sea. The Picts (now the chief tribe of Scotland) made a fierce raid on Hadrian's Wall and broke through. At the same time the north-west coast was invaded by Scots, a Celtic tribe from Ireland who afterwards settled in the country that bears their name. The unfortunate Romans, caught in a three-pronged attack, suffered a crushing defeat. The Count of the Saxon Shore, head of coastal defences, was killed, along with many of his forces. Dozens of villas were destroyed, thousands of slaves were set free and large areas of farmland were damaged.

Roman Britain never fully recovered from these invasions, although a determined effort was made to rebuild its defences. In the following spring, when most of the barbarians had been pushed back, the work of restoring the frontier wall began. This time there were no milecastles or turrets. All the troops, together with their families, lived in the repaired forts. Along the north-east coast (in the area of present-day Yorkshire) stone signal towers were built as a defence against sea raids. Remains of these have been found at Filey, Scarborough and other places further north.

The legions go home

By this time Rome itself was in danger. Barbarian invasions along the Rhine and Danube frontiers were straining the defences of the Empire to breaking point (see Chapter 44). More and more soldiers

Decoration on a box made
by the Franks—'barbarians'
who overran Roman Gaul
in the fifth century

had to be withdrawn from the outer provinces, including Britain, to
defend the heart of the Empire. As a result, the tribes from Scotland
could not be held back. In about 383 Hadrian's Wall was again
overrun by Picts and others. This time there was no attempt to rebuild it. There were not enough troops to man all the forts properly
in any case. Within a few years the signal stations on the Yorkshire
coast were also abandoned.

As the Empire grew weaker, it became impossible for the Roman
government to protect a province as far away as Britain. Eventually,
in 410, the Britons were told that they would have to defend themselves as best they could. This was the year in which Alaric the Goth
successfully attacked Rome, and it was probably the time when the
last Roman legion left Britain. No Roman coin dating from a later
period has been found in the British Isles.

Possibly the Romans hoped to come back to Britain if they could
defeat the barbarians. It seems that the Britons were anxious for
them to return and help defend the country against its enemies,
especially the sea raiders. We know they had not given up hope as
late as 446, because in that year a number of leading Britons sent an
appeal to Rome. It said: 'The barbarians thrust us into the sea, the
sea pushes us back to the barbarians; we are either murdered or we
drown.'

But no help came. By the middle of the fifth century Britain was a
lost province, even though many of its people still had a feeling of
belonging to the Roman Empire. The pagan Angles and Saxons

from Germany had started to overrun the country and settle on the land—mainly in the lowland areas of the south-east. Villas and even whole towns became deserted, as the Britons fled westwards to escape the invaders. Many of those that stayed behind were killed or enslaved.

What the Romans did for Britain

A large part of Britain had been a province of the Roman Empire for roughly 350 years. However the effects of Roman occupation varied greatly between the north and the south and between rich and poor people. Peasant farmers, especially those in the 'military areas' of the north and west, had very little contact with the Romans. Some sold corn, meat and hides at markets which grew up round the forts. This may have enabled them to purchase small quantities of Roman pottery or metal-ware. But otherwise their way of life hardly changed.

In the peaceful south-east, on the other hand, many people lived just like the Romans in Italy—especially if they were wealthy. Towns and trade developed and people learned Latin, wore Roman clothes, had Roman furniture and decorations in their homes, and often worshipped Roman gods as well. But it was this *Romanised* area that suffered the full force of the Anglo-Saxon invasions. The new settlers made no attempt to carry on Roman customs. They lived a simple village life, allowing the deserted towns to crumble, the roads to decay and Roman knowledge to be forgotten. Even the Christian religion began to disappear.

The Fosse Way today. You can see that the Romans made their roads as straight as possible

Nevertheless, a few traces of the Roman occupation remained. Even today, the routes of many main roads are almost the same as those laid down by the legions. It was in the Roman period that London first developed as an important centre of trade and the natural capital of Britain. Furthermore, the fact that the Romans had been in the country may in some way explain why the Angles and Saxons that came to Britain soon became more advanced than those that stayed behind in northern Europe.

Questions

PART ONE

Chapter 1

  1   From what kind of animal has man descended?

  2   How did early man make stone tools and what did he use them for?

  3   How did speaking help early man?

Chapter 2

  4   What animals were hunted by early man? How did he kill them?

  5   What was the purpose of cave drawings?

Chapter 3

  6   Why did many hunters dislike the idea of farming?

  7   Describe some of the earliest farming methods.

  8   Give three important achievements of the peoples of the New Stone Age.

  9   Why did most early men worship a goddess rather than a god?

Chapter 4

10   What is irrigation?

11   As far as we know, what was the first metal discovered by man?

12   Give as many reasons as you can why early farmers lived near water.

Chapter 5

13   Explain the meanings of the following: sarsens, bluestones, trilithons, heelstone.

14   For what reasons is it likely that Stonehenge was built?

PART TWO

Chapter 6

15   Give the four names by which the 'Land between Rivers' has been known.

16   Why is Sumerian writing called 'cuneiform'?

17   What was a ziggurat?

18   How have the Babylonians affected present-day counting?

Chapter 7

19   From the laws of Hammurabi, write down the one you think the fairest and the one you think the most unfair.

20   What did the Babylonians use palm trees for?

Chapter 8

21   Why were the Assyrians thought to be the cruellest people of ancient times?

22   What was Nineveh like in the time of Sennacherib?

23   Describe the library of Assurbanipal.

24   Why did the Assyrian Empire collapse?

25   (*a*) Describe the Hanging Gardens of Babylon.

       (*b*) How did they get their name?

PART THREE

Chapter 9

26   What were the 'treasures' which Howard Carter found in Tutankhamen's tomb?

27   Why were the inundations important to the Egyptians?

Chapter 24
59 For what purpose did the Greeks consult the priestess at Delphi?
60 Name two events in the ancient Olympic Games which are not held in the modern Olympics.
61 Why were successful athletes honoured by the Greeks?

Chapter 25
62 Give the names of two Persian Kings who invaded Greece and two battles they fought.
63 How did the present-day Marathon Race get its name?
64 According to Herodotus, how big was Xerxes' army and how did he count it?

Chapter 26
65 Describe the Battle of Salamis in your own words.
66 In what way were the Greeks lucky to win the Battle of Plataea?

Chapter 27
67 Describe Greek democracy.
68 (*a*) Who was the great leader of Athens after the Persian Wars?
    (*b*) What did he do to make Athens great?
69 (*a*) What was the Parthenon?
    (*b*) How was it built?

Chapter 28
70 How was Ancient Greece a 'man's world'?
71 In what ways was Greek education different from that of today?
72 Describe one important craft in Athens.

Chapter 29
73 Describe a typical Greek theatre.
74 Give the names of three Greek philosophers and write a sentence about each.
75 What discovery is Archimedes famous for?

Chapter 30
76 Why was Athens defeated in the Peloponnesian War?
77 How did Philip of Macedon make his army 'unbeatable'?
78 Describe the character of Alexander the Great.

Chapter 31
79 Name the three battles in which Alexander destroyed the power of the Persians.
80 Why was Alexander forced to turn back when he reached India?
81 (*a*) Where and when did Alexander die?
    (*b*) What happened to his empire after his death?
82 In what ways did Alexander influence the peoples he conquered?

PART EIGHT

Chapter 32
83 In what ways was Rome in a good geographical position?
84 (*a*) How were the Etruscans and the Greeks different from the Latin tribes?
    (*b*) Why did Josiah Wedgwood call his factory Etruria?
85 According to the legend, how many kings ruled Rome between 753 and 509 B.C.? Name two of them.

Chapter 33
86 List the meanings of the following words: republic, consuls, veto, Senate, patricians, plebeians, tribunes.
87 Why did the plebeians think they were being treated unfairly? How did they protest?
88 In what ways did the plebeians achieve a more equal position in Rome?

Chapter 34
89 (*a*) How were the first armies of Rome recruited?
    (*b*) Why were wars short in this period?

90 Why are we unsure of much of Rome's history before 390 B.C.?
91 What is meant by a 'Pyrrhic victory'? Explain the origin of the phrase.
92 What sorts of traffic used roads like the Appian Way?

Chapter 35
93 How did the Carthaginians become rich and powerful?
94 How did the Romans manage to fight a 'land battle at sea'?
95 Why was Hannibal unable to conquer Rome?

Chapter 36
96 (*a*) What were the duties of a provincial governor?
     (*b*) How did many of them grow rich?
97 In what ways did the peasants of Italy suffer as a result of Rome's foreign conquests?
98 (*a*) Why were the common people dissatisfied with the rule of the Senate?
     (*b*) Name *two* of their leaders.

Chapter 37
99 How did Marius reorganise the Roman army and its legions?
100 Describe *three* of Rome's 'troubles' in the first half of the first century B.C.
101 (*a*) What was Julius Caesar's great ambition?
      (*b*) Explain how he achieved it.

Chapter 38
102 Which months of the year are named after Roman rulers?
103 Why was Julius Caesar murdered?
104 Why did Antony and Octavian quarrel with each other?
105 Mention *two* ways in which Augustus was a successful ruler.

Chapter 39
106 How were the achievements of Trajan different from those of Hadrian?
107 In what ways was Rome 'a city of contrasts'?
108 How could strangers find their way around Rome?
109 Which places in Rome were busiest
      (*a*) in the morning,
      (*b*) in the afternoon?
110 Name *two* Roman entertainments which attracted large crowds.

Chapter 40
111 How was marriage in Roman times different from marriage today?
112 (*a*) Give as many examples as you can of work done by slaves.
      (*b*) Why were slaves so often ill-treated?
113 (*a*) What was a toga?
      (*b*) Why were the early Romans proud to wear togas?

Chapter 41
114 Why did most Romans go to bed early?
115 Explain the meanings of the following: *atrium, impluvium, peristyle hypocaust,* mosaic, villa.
116 How were Roman eating habits different from ours today?

Chapter 42
117 Find *three* important differences between education today and in Roman times.
118 Why was *oratory* such an important school subject?
119 What was
      (*a*) parchment,
      (*b*) a stylus,
      (*c*) a volume?
120 Name *three* Roman writers.

Chapter 43
121 What were the Roman gods of the household?
122 Why did Christians get into trouble with the Roman government?
123 Explain the meanings of the following words: *Messiah,* disciples, persecution, catacombs, Pope, pagans.

Further Reading

D. R. Barker, *The Story of Ancient Athens* (Edward Arnold).

H. Baumann, *The World of the Pharaohs* (O.U.P.).

C. A. Burland, *Ancient China; Ancient Egypt; Ancient Greece;* and *Ancient Rome* (Hulton, Great Civilisations series).

R. Carrington, *Ancient Egypt; Ancient Greece; Ancient Rome;* and *Ancient Sumer* (Chatto & Windus, Dawn of History series).

R. Fawcett, ed., *India;* and *Sumer* (P. R. Gawthorn, How Did They Live series).

R. Fawcett, *Persia* (Bruce & Gawthorn, What Was Their Life series).

A. Fox and A. Sorrell, *Roman Britain* (Lutterworth).

History Jackdaw No. 41, *Hadrian's Wall* (Cape).

E. G. Hume, *Days Before History* (Blackie, the Pilgrim's Way, Book 1).

M. MacGregor, *The Story of Rome* (Nelson).

Ray Mitchell, *Roman Britain* (Longman, Focus on History series).

Jane Osborn, *Stone Age to Iron Age* (Longman, Focus on History series).

D. Taylor, *A Soldier on Hadrian's Wall* (O.U.P., People of the Past series).

A. F. Titterton, *Before the Norman Conquest* (Ginn's History Bookshelves, Blue Shelf).

A. F. Titterton and K. M. Gadd, *Ancient Civilisations* (Ginn, Looking at the Past series).

R. J. Unstead, *People in History,* Book 1 (A. and C. Black). Includes Caratacus, Boudicca, Agricola and St Alban.

V. White, *A Romano-British Family* (O.U.P., People of the Past series).

Longman Then and There series includes:

G. W. Barrett, *Ancient China.*

James Bolton, *Ancient Crete and Mycenae.*

Joan Liversidge, *Roman Britain.*

Naomi Mitchison, *Alexander the Great.*

Robin Place, *Prehistoric Britain.*

E. J. Sheppard, *Ancient Athens; Ancient Egypt.*

N. Sherwin-White, *Ancient Rome.*

Thomson, Oliver, *The Romans in Scotland.*

Weidenfeld and Nicolson Young Historian Series includes:

R. L. Green, *Ancient Greece, Ancient Egypt.*

H. E. L. Mellersh, *Imperial Rome.*

E. R. Pike, *Ancient India, Lands of the Bible, Republican Rome.*

C. Spencer, *Ancient China.*

Filmstrips

Filmstrips are in colour unless otherwise stated.

'Digging for History' (*Daily Mail;* distributed by the Educational Foundation for Visual Aids). Black and white.

'People Before History' (Hulton). Black and white.

'Living Before History': Part 1 — Cave men and Hunters; Part 2 — Farmers and Craftsmen (Common Ground).

'Life in Ancient Mesopotamia' (*The Ancient World,* Common Ground).

'Ancient Babylonia' (Hulton). Black and white.

'Life in Ancient Egypt' (*The Ancient World,* Common Ground).

'The Story of the Pyramids' (Tartan; distributed by John King). Black and white.

'The Greeks' (Educational Productions).

'The Olympic Games' (Carwal). With recorded commentary on 4-inch tape.

'Alexander the Great' (Tartan; distributed by John King). Black and white.

'The Growth of Rome' (*The Ancient World,* Common Ground).

'The Romans' (Educational Productions).

'Pompeii' (Edita; distributed by Rank).

'Hannibal'
'Julius Caesar' } (Fabbri; distributed by Hulton).

'The Romans in Britain' (Educational Productions).

'The Roman Wall' (Hulton; in association with Gateway). Black and white.

Index

Page numbers in **bold** type denote illustrations